BEYOND THE ECHO CHAMBER

BEYOND THE ECHO CHAMBER

Reshaping Politics Through Networked Progressive Media

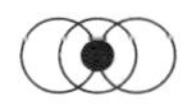

JESSICA CLARK
and
TRACY VAN SLYKE

THE NEW PRESS
NEW YORK
LONDON

Published in the United States by The New Press, New York, 2010
Distributed by W. W. Norton & Company, Inc., New York

LIBRARY OF CONGRESS CATALOGING-IN-PUBLICATION DATA

Clark, Jessica.
Beyond the echo chamber : reshaping politics through networked progressive media / Jessica Clark and Tracy Van Slyke.
p. cm.
Includes bibliographical references and index.
ISBN 978-1-59558-471-7 (pbk. : alk. paper) 1. Mass media--Political aspects—United States—History—21st century. 2. Online journalism—Political aspects—United States—History—21st century. 3. United States—Politics and government—2001–2009. I. Van Slyke, Tracy. II. Title.
P95.82.U6C53 2010
302.230973—dc22 2009037840

The New Press was established in 1990 as a not-for-profit alternative to the large, commercial publishing houses currently dominating the book publishing industry. The New Press operates in the public interest rather than for private gain, and is committed to publishing, in innovative ways, works of educational, cultural, and community value that are often deemed insufficiently profitable.

www.thenewpress.com

Composition by The Influx House
This book was set in Kievit and Janson Text

Printed in the United States of America

10 9 8 7 6 5 4 3 2 1

We'd like to dedicate this book to our husbands, Dan and Spoon—who put up with, cooked for, and stuck with us during countless work-filled nights and weekends—and to our parents, who inspired us to be passionate about the world.

CONTENTS

ACKNOWLEDGMENTS

Over the course of the four years that it took us to research and write this book, we sought help from many quarters. Thanks to Pat Aufderheide and the Ford Foundation for supporting Jessica's research via the Center for Social Media. Thanks to The Media Consortium for allowing Tracy to not only write about progressive media but also support it. We appreciate the invaluable research and editing assistance provided by Brian Cook, Christine Cupaiuolo, Katie Donnelly, Brandon Forbes, and Anna Grace Schneider. Thanks to our readers: your comments made the book stronger. (Our favorite one: "It reads like a thriller!") We began this work at *In These Times* magazine and send a shout-out to all of the friends and colleagues who passed through those doors. And thanks to all of you creative, feisty progressive media makers out there who have made these some of the most interesting years of our lives.

BEYOND THE ECHO CHAMBER

SECTION I:
LAYING THE GROUNDWORK

INTRODUCTION

On May 10, 2007, investigative reporter Jeremy Scahill and documentary film producer Robert Greenwald testified before Congress on the role of private contractors in the war on Iraq. Both had already spent many months investigating how and why a shadow force of soldiers-for-hire was being allowed to fight alongside U.S. troops for more pay, with less oversight.

"Many Americans are under the impression that the U.S. currently has about 145,000 active duty troops on the ground in Iraq," Scahill testified. His *New York Times* bestselling book, *Blackwater: The Rise of the World's Most Powerful Mercenary Army*, emerged from a series of articles supported by The Nation Institute and published for *The Nation*, America's oldest left-leaning magazine. "What is seldom mentioned is the fact that there are at least 126,000 private personnel deployed alongside the official armed forces. These private forces effectively double the size of the occupation force, largely without the knowledge of the U.S. taxpayers that foot the bill."[1]

Greenwald, who directed the 2006 film *Iraq for Sale: The War Profiteers*, invoked the many personal stories uncovered by his research team at Brave New Films, the production company he founded in 2004. He described how U.S. Army SPC David Mann, a radio repair technician who served in Iraq, was forced to train private contractors from the corporation KBR to replace him. Stewart Scott, a former employee for Halliburton (another corporation employed in Iraq by the U.S. government), revealed that contractors had stayed in five-star hotels while U.S. soldiers slept on the ground. "We know corporations are designed to create significant returns for shareholders," said Greenwald. "Do we really believe they can and should be fighting for hearts and minds?"[2]

The presence of Scahill and Greenwald in front of the House Appropriations Subcommittee on Defense revealed that the independent, progressive media had broken through to Capitol Hill on a critical matter of national defense policy. The debate in Congress eventually led to provisions in the 2008 Defense Authorization Bill that would tighten government oversight of private security contractors working in Iraq and Afghanistan, requiring clear rules of engagement for private guards and establishing minimum standards for hiring and training them. The contractors would also have to comply with military regulations and orders issued by commanders in a war zone. President George W. Bush vetoed the bill in December 2007. But the issue could not be stopped. By December 2008, Scahill reported, six Blackwater operatives had either been indicted on or pled guilty to manslaughter charges related to the shooting deaths of Iraqi civilians.[3] In May 2009, a Senate hearing revealed that the Department of Defense had paid KBR more than $80 million in bonuses to install substandard wiring at U.S. bases in Iraq that may have caused the death of up to eighteen U.S. soldiers.[4]

Without in-depth reporting and powerful storytelling to forcefully drive it, the issue of military contractors never would have sparked such contentious political debate. A reporter testifying before Congress may not seem remarkable, but this is one among a series of critical moments that together mark a new era for explicitly left-leaning media makers.

Some, like Scahill, worked their way up through the ranks of openly partisan outlets such as *Democracy Now!* and *The Nation*, following the muckraking tradition of Upton Sinclair and I.F. Stone. Others, like Greenwald, left lucrative commercial careers, spurred by a sense of outrage and urgency. Collectively, their choices have paid off: from magazines to blogs, documentary films to YouTube videos, national radio stations to podcasts, media that loosely identify themselves as "progressive" are more visible and influential than ever before.

WHAT'S PROGRESSIVE MEDIA, ANYWAY?

Such media projects span both old and new platforms, drawing upon a variety of political perspectives and rhetorical strategies. In the chapters that follow, we focus largely on projects and outlets that offer journalism and political commentary, rather than media produced by campaigns, advertisers, or political advocacy groups—although it's worth noting that the boundaries have blurred significantly online.

The term "progressive" has its historical basis in political movements and parties from the turn of the twentieth century. At its root is the idea of social progress, as opposed to conservative philosophies that seek to maintain older systems of value and power. Revived, the term served a number of functions as it entered the general lexicon over the course of the Bush administration. "Progressive" distinguished followers from wimpy "liberals," signaling a political identity that was left of center but not fundamentally radical, and provided a rallying cry for a younger group of (big-*D* and little-*d*) democratic activists. A 2005 article from the Web site Campus Progress offers a working definition:

> "At its core," John Halpin, senior advisor on the staff of [D.C.-based think tank] the Center for American Progress writes, "progressivism is a non-ideological, pragmatic system of thought grounded in solving problems and maintaining strong values within society." Progressivism is practical and driven by the values that define America morality and have made our country stronger and better. It's a dynamic concept giving the leadership of an up-and-coming genera-

> tion of politicos—you—the tools to make this nation's future brighter for all.[5]

Nate Silver of the political analysis Web site FiveThirtyEight.com offered a useful comparison between "rational progressivism" and "radical progressivism."[6] Rational progressives, he wrote, tend to be reform- and outcome-oriented, seeking synthetic solutions informed by empirical evidence and a technocratic mind-set. In contrast, radical progressives seek social and political transformation, orient themselves ideologically in terms of economic philosophy or identity issues, and understand politics as a battle of wills rather than a battle of ideas.

"Rational progressives sometimes regard radical progressives as impractical, self-righteous, shrill, demagogic, naive and/or anti-intellectual. Radical progressives, in turn, regard rational progressives as impure, corrupt (or corruptible), selfish, complacent, elitist, and too quick to compromise," wrote Silver.

As this description suggests, many people relate to the term in different ways, and often not with kindness (even if they fall on the left end of the political spectrum). But that's another book. Here we will be focusing on media outlets that have, from 2004 to the present, identified as progressive and made a mark on the political conversation. We recognize and admire the many other media projects that serve valuable social functions—including public media, arts and culture productions, international news outlets, and more—but we've limited our research here to the evolution of U. S.-based, networked, high-impact progressive media.

These progressive media outlets shape current debates, inform and activate millions of people, and create long-lasting change in American society. Their force comes from hundreds of individual editors, reporters, bloggers, reporter/bloggers, producers, and pundits who choose to risk career and credibility to speak truth to power.

In the months following 9/11, such critical voices were shut out of both the mainstream media discussion and the halls of Congress. But as the unmitigated fiasco of George W. Bush's administration wore on, a series of profound political and technological shocks both reenergized then-marginal left-leaning print and broadcast projects and spawned a dynamic new breed of independent media outlets and citizen producers.

Unlike their commercial counterparts, progressive media makers aren't motivated primarily by profit or audience share. Instead, they're drawn to their work by passion and mission: to shed light on corrupt government and corporate actions, strike back against conservative ideologues, and give voice to the voiceless.

Despite right-wing caricatures of the "radical left," progressive media and their creators are far from monolithic. Many have different missions and means for their work. Some projects report critically on politicians, activists, and advocacy groups; others work alongside them to develop campaigns, frames, and debate fodder. Some are recognized and funded by inside-the-Beltway power brokers; others have to struggle for dollars and airtime.

Identifying and assessing the impact of such efforts can be tricky; no single yardstick applies, especially in this moment of quick-shifting technologies and tactics. But the survival of both these projects and our democracy rests on a better understanding of how such media work to change minds and policies.

Progressive media engage significant swaths of the population in politics and help to energize and inform national and international debates. Progressive media also demonstrate the shallowness of the safe and toothless "he said/she said" establishment journalism, providing a counterweight to dominance of the airwaves by conservative pundits.

In *Echo Chamber: Rush Limbaugh and the Conservative Media Establishment*, scholars Kathleen Hall Jamieson and Joseph N. Cappella made the case for the virtues of partisan media. "History sides with the notion that one-sided partisan communication produces engagement," they wrote. What's more, when coherently framed and argued, partisan structures "make it easier for those holding them to make sense of new information." Partisan media help to hold mainstream journalists accountable, and "arm their audience to argue effectively."[7] Finally, they help to create a sense of community, even among members who might not agree on all fronts.

But while the conservative echo chamber served its members well through much of the Bush years, we'd argue that progressives have surpassed this model to build something better.

In the early years of the Bush administration, both citizen and legacy media makers were struggling to build a progressive media infrastructure that could rival the right's coordinated echo chamber, which successfully disseminated talking points (and talking heads) via print, talk radio, cable television, and mainstream news outlets. As it turns out, this top-down lockstep model didn't work for progressive media makers, who are still learning to move "beyond the echo chamber" to find new pathways to impact and influence. In the chapters that follow, we describe the transformation of the progressive media sphere from an atomized, isolated collection of struggling one-to-many outlets to a vibrant network spanning engaged citizens, multiplatform outlets, influential issue campaigns, and innovative reporting projects.

What's our stake in all of this? We aren't disinterested observers. Both of us spent the better part of the Bush years producing, managing, fighting for, and critiquing independent and progressive media. We met in 2004 at *In These Times* magazine, where Jessica was the managing editor and Tracy was hired as associate publisher. By the time we both left in 2007, Jessica was the executive editor, Tracy was the publisher, and we'd revamped the magazine and its Web site, winning an *Utne Reader* award for Best Political Reporting in the process. After leaving the magazine, Tracy went on to head up a network of progressive media outlets called The Media Consortium (more on that to follow), while Jessica went on to lead the Future of Public Media Project at

American University's Center for Social Media. We both believe deeply that the mission of our democracy is not only to propel the successful into more success but also to provide a support system and launching pad for the disenfranchised—and that media are central to that mission.

We spoke with numerous media makers about their strategies and challenges over the past several years, and you'll hear their voices throughout this book. The profiles and interviews featured in this book reflect our own curiosity about what works, what doesn't, and what to try next. Along the way, we explore how the progressive media sector evolved during Bush's final term, unpacking high-impact moments and case studies for evidence of how to assess and achieve progressive media successes. There are dozens of valuable progressive media outlets and sources, and while we couldn't cover them all in this book due to its framework, we want to underscore that a cumulative progressive media network is a vital component of a long-lasting progressive majority.

While not all progressive media projects deal with electoral politics, we chose to analyze changes over one presidential election cycle because dollars and media makers tend to flow into progressive outlets based on national shifts in power. As it happened, this cycle also offered historic highs and lows: the resignation of several high-profile conservative officials, a midterm Democratic victory in Congress, a devastating natural disaster exacerbated by a woeful government response, a popular backlash against anti-immigration forces, unprecedented presidential campaigns by female and minority candidates, and a looming economic crisis the likes of which the country had not seen in decades.

But our goal in examining this transformative period is to serve not as historians but as investigators, in search of clues that reveal successful strategies for progressive media makers and projects.

How did progressive bloggers and traditional journalists learn to work together? How did single-platform outlets engage in high-impact multiplatform campaigns that cross multiple activist networks? How did *you* become a central component of an ever-evolving, 24/7 networked progressive media sector that creates social and political change?

Read on.

1
SETTING THE STAGE FOR CHANGE

The start of Bush's first term in 2000 marked significant shifts in the political and technological landscapes, laying the foundation for an explosion of progressive media outlets in the 2004–8 cycle. What made the first four years of the century so critical to the evolution of progressive media?

The 2000 election was a pivotal turning point for both the American left and the larger public, demonstrating how central journalism could be to democracy. Mainstream cable outlets played a major role in exacerbating the confusion around the election. Early estimates from the Voter News Service—an exit-polling consortium set up by the television networks and the Associated Press—called Florida for Democratic candidate Al Gore. But it was the Fox News desk, led by Bush's first cousin John Ellis, who called the state for the Republican candidate. As other networks followed suit, Gore conceded, making it difficult to rebound when serious questions about the tally surfaced.[1] Progressive outlets such as *Mother Jones*, AlterNet, and TomPaine.com leapt in to investigate, and an initial wave of political bloggers—capitalizing on newly forged online publishing tools—jumped into the critical fray. While they weren't able to avert Bush's eventual victory, these media makers focused attention and pressure on the broken electoral system.

As much as they failed in Florida in 2000, the domestic establishment media reached its nadir in the wake of the 9/11 attacks.

"Between the War on Terror and the war with Iraq, the Bush White House all but guaranteed itself a timid press corps that emphasized its megaphone function," wrote media critic Eric Boehlert in his 2006 book, *Lapdogs: How the Press Rolled Over for Bush.*[2] "The MSM [mainstream media] coverage of the War on Terror and their reporting during the run-up to the invasion of Iraq were inexorably linked. By the time the invasion was launched in March of 2003, the press was so comfortable having spent the previous year lying down for the White House and its foreboding War on Terror, that it could not muster enough energy to get up off the floor."

But what the mainstream media were afraid to do, the progressive, independent media were not. Audiences turned to alternative sources of news and critical analysis, helping to catalyze the next phase of growth for the progressive media sector.

By the end of 2003, faced with the failed invasion of Afghanistan and the Bush administration's spurious claims of "Mission Accomplished" in Iraq, a new generation of citizen media makers sprang into action. Just as the online organizing group MoveOn had seized on e-mail and the Web in the late 1990s to organize responses to the Clinton impeachment, bloggers such as Markos Moulitsas, founder of the now enormously popular left-wing blog Daily Kos, took advantage of new online tools to openly critique both the Bush administration's flawed war and the Democrats' failures to block it.

"Perhaps nothing is fueling the rise of the a new progressive movement more than the lack of urgency from the Democratic political establishment in D.C. Twelve years after Newt Gingrich and his Contract with America helped sweep Democrats into a political Siberia, the Democratic Party and its coalition of single-issue groups and its consultant class continue to act as if the party still holds a majority. . . . If progressives want to win now, it is up to the new people-powered movement to get active," wrote Moulitsas and co-author Jerome Armstrong, one of the founding members of the progressive political blogosphere with the blog MyDD.com, in their 2006 book *Crashing the Gate: Netroots, Grassroots and the Rise of People-Powered Politics.*[3]

This period also marked a moment of experimentation for print progressive outlets. Many were still trying to adjust their business and publishing models to account for the shift from paper to pixels, and participatory media tools added another layer of complication. As the administration racked up more gaffes and atrocities that the mainstream media failed to challenge, popular interest kept escalating, raising the circulation and visibility of existing legacy outlets such as *Mother Jones*, the *American Prospect*, *The Nation*, *In These Times*, *Washington Monthly*, the *Utne Reader*, and *The Progressive*, and racking up new audiences for that cadre of progressive bloggers that became known as the "netroots."

"Progressives were angry not just with the media but also with Democratic Party leaders for their unwillingness to challenge the Bush administration's case for war," wrote Lakshmi Chaudhry in a 2006 analysis of the bloggers' rise published in *In These Times.*[4] "That much-touted liberal rage found its expression on blogs like Eschaton, Daily Kos and Talking Points Memo, and continues to fuel the phenomenal growth of the progressive blogosphere. Like the rise of right-wing talk radio, this growth is directly linked to an institutional failure of representation. Finding no mirror for their views in the media, a large segment of the American public turned to the Internet to speak for themselves—often with brutal, uncensored candor."

Documentaries also experienced a renaissance as a result of the mainstream narrowing of news. Just before the 2004 election, the outspoken, award-winning progressive filmmaker Michael Moore released *Fahrenheit 9/11*—a barnstorming indictment of the administration's ties to Saudi Arabia and the bin Laden family, designed to shed doubt on Bush's response to 9/11. The film won the top prize at Cannes, and despite a concentrated conservative campaign pressuring theater owners not to screen it, the opening weekend broke a record set by *Rocky III* for a film opening in fewer than a thousand theaters. MoveOn members helped Moore reach this benchmark; more than a hundred thousand pledged to see the film when it first opened.[5]

Mainstream critics lambasted Moore for his polemic style, but audiences didn't mind. While Moore failed in his ultimate goal of cementing Bush's defeat in the election, the film's success revealed to politicos and the commercial media world that there was a large audience of progressives and angry independents hungry for aggressively partisan media to counter what former conservative David Brock dubbed the "Republican Noise Machine" in his influential 2004 book of the same name.[6]

Strategically constructed over the last three decades, that machine was in full swing during this time. For years, the left forlornly admired the structure and dominance of the right-wing media, well financed by conservative foundations, and even in some cases profitable. Conservatives had taken advantage of emerging markets—cable and satellite television, talk radio—to establish popular, high-profile stations, programs, and personalities. The right-wing media infrastructure was designed in a top-down manner, allowing the individual outlets and allies to cumulatively swarm the news cycle and dominate establishment punditry. While the right publicly accused the mainstream media of being "liberal," it was the right that in fact had come to dominate the analysis.

Though the "noise machine" moniker caught on, Brock wasn't the first to notice it—media monitors at organizations such as Fairness and Accuracy in Reporting (FAIR) had been tracking its growth since the mid-1980s, and right-wing bias in mainstream media was a mainstay topic for left-wing journals of opinion. As the *American Prospect*'s Robert Borosage wrote in 2002:

> With all that ideological money, institutional heft, coordination, and credentialing, the right has perfected what the CIA used to call a "mighty Wurlitzer"—a propaganda machine

> that can hone a fact or a lie, broadcast it, and have it echoed and recycled in Fox News commentary, in *Washington Times* news stories, in *Wall Street Journal* editorials, by myriad right-wing pundits, by Heritage seminars and briefing papers, and in congressional hearings and speeches. . . . There is nothing on the progressive side of town remotely competitive with this. There is no progressive TV network and few progressive pundits. Several good journals of opinion exist, but nothing with the reach of Rush Limbaugh, the *Journal* editorial page, Rupert Murdoch's Fox News network, or even the *Washington Times*.[7]

From 2000 to 2004, the power and influence of conservative media outlets, think tanks, and pundits was examined and laid bare, especially within the context of their dominance of television networks, radio airwaves, and newspaper opinion pages.

In 2004, Robert Greenwald, riding the newly empowered wave of political documentary, tackled one of the loudest members of the conservatives' noise machine. His documentary *Outfoxed: Rupert Murdoch's War on Journalism* was a no-holds-barred feature-length critique of Fox News. The film revealed the hypocrisy of the cable channel unabashedly touting itself as "Fair and Balanced" despite cornering the market on right-wing propaganda. While left-leaning media critics had been slagging Fox for years, Greenwald and his team at Brave New Films effectively combined investigation with organizing and guerilla marketing, creating an innovative online and offline distribution strategy that hooked in dozens of organizational allies and progressive journalism outlets and harnessed MoveOn's engaged online membership. (We cover this in more detail in Chapter 5, "Fight the Right.")

The film created a resounding feedback loop. Traditional mainstream media outlets were fascinated by the director's strategy and the audience response. The resulting coverage forced Fox to respond and attack, generating yet more media attention.

The new online and offline distribution routines pioneered by Greenwald also informed strategies for a stream of high-profile political documentaries, including Al Gore's 2006 *An Inconvenient Truth*, which sparked a global reassessment of the gravity of the climate crisis. The successful campaign around *Outfoxed* also reinforced the fact that certain segments of the progressive media could go aggressively on the offensive—contradicting cultural narratives about ineffective and wimpy liberals.

For many progressive observers at the time, the question was: How would the left continue to parry the conservative media drumbeat?

Different factions of the resurging progressive media sector had different solutions. Brock's book inspired fund-raiser Rob Stein to create a PowerPoint presentation documenting the rise and coordination of the right-wing political and media infrastructure. Stein's talks to large groups of liberal donors led to the formation of the Democracy Alliance—a group of the largest liberal donors in the country, with a shared goal of creating a progressive infrastructure to rival that of the right. A new consensus was emerging: progressives needed their own echo chamber, fast.

COMPETING PHILOSOPHIES

But while the right had decades to successfully craft a powerful and well-oiled infrastructure that spread and built upon its ideology, progressives were scrambling to construct a counterpoint within a few years. And the plan to mirror "the mighty Wurlitzer" was met with resistance from traditional journalists and editors associated with progressive outlets, who protested the rush to speak in one voice. Their proposed solution to the "noise machine" problem was to fund more investigation and reporting, filling in for mainstream journalism outlets weakened by consolidation, sinking ad revenues, and conservative bullying.

In contrast, members of the political blogosphere, using online tools to build their own networks and funding streams, found little common cause with legacy progressive outlets during this period. Instead, they focused their critique on mainstream outlets and their efforts on building their own intersecting infrastructure, bolstered by the use of online outreach and fund-raising in Howard Dean's 2004 presidential run.

None of these strategies was necessarily better or the right answer; instead, they reflected the strengths of each of the sectors proposing them. As it turned out, a more connected progressive media network emerged that did not quite mirror the right but instead played up the strengths of the left. (We dive into that in Chapter 4, "Build Network-Powered Media.") But competition still reigned, and it would take some experiments, failures, and, before long, successes for these different parts to start working in concert.

In the broadcast world, the March 2004 launch of Air America Radio represented one high-profile and controversial antidote to the right-wing dominance of talk radio by polemic hosts such as Rush Limbaugh and Michael Savage. Eschewing both the measured reporting of National Public Radio and the often sober and sometimes scholastic tone of progressive magazines such as the *American Prospect* or *The Nation*, the fledgling network adopted a barnstorming and sometimes comedic tone in many of its programs. Since its inception, Air America has seen its fair share of ups and downs, including multiple owners, bankruptcy filings, internal spats, and external criticisms.

But Air America has provided a home and platform for many of today's progressive political superstars, allowing them to break through into mainstream outlets: from Cenk Uygar (who has hosted a number of commercially viable online and on-air progressive programs) and Rachel Maddow (who was named as the host of her own highly successful nighttime show on MSNBC in summer 2008) to Al Franken, now a Minnesota senator. Air America is one of a cluster of national outlets that have helped to define and nurture high-impact progressive personalities.

Air America represented just one in a series of infrastructure-building efforts within the progressive media sector. While conservative donors and foundations had invested heavily in a coordinated ideological and media infrastructure, traditional left media outlets were working in isolation, often without high-level support from leading liberal donors and foundations. In 2005, we tracked the differences between the right and left media infrastructures in a map published in *In These Times* (see pp. 18–19). The map revealed scarce foundation support for progressive media outlets, gaps in communication between the Beltway and the grassroots, and a lack of coherent talking points.

Much to our surprise, the map itself became a tool for organizing the progressive media network. We heard through the grapevine that it was taped to organizations' walls, brought to funders to make the case for more support, and requested by the campaign of 2004 presidential candidate Wesley Clark. We found that we weren't alone in our frustrations.

THE PROGRESSIVE SURGE

The rise of the new network accompanied that of a new political identity: the "progressive." While this term has since become muddied, at the time it represented both a generational break and an ideological one. Many of this younger set of media producers felt little or no connection to the movements of the sixties and seventies that were still feeding the perspective and operations of the traditional left press. They also saw the limitations of the identity-based politics of the eighties and nineties. The political tactics of previous generations—such as the large street-level protests that had failed to garner significant coverage or reaction in the first years of the Iraq invasion—were no longer working. A certain pragmatism marked this new wave of political activists, coupled with a focus on opportunity over the much-maligned "liberal" preference for entitlements. The online space opened up new possibilities for changing the tone and pace of media and analysis and for pioneering new forms of political organizing and movement building. Suddenly, the generation that had been dismissed as slackers found themselves on the leading edge of political change.

New roles began to emerge within the sector, with progressive think tanks providing policy fodder, progressive reporters steadily investigating scandals, and bloggers watchdogging the mainstream outlets and amplifying talking points. While ostensibly nonpartisan, humorists such as Jon Stewart of *The Daily Show* had broken through the post-9/11 timidity to critique both the war and the Bush administration. Documentary films were serving as vehicles for moving controversial issues into the national debate, and tough progressive voices had begun to drown out the so-called milquetoast liberal views so skewered by right-wing mouthpieces such as Ann Coulter. Howard Dean was whipping up unprecedented enthusiasm and donations via the Web. Political 527 campaigns were countering Republican "swiftboating" and attack ads in key media markets. And online tools were offering individuals and already-in-the mix media organizations new chances to act as political power brokers, message machines, mobilizers, fundraisers, instant fact checkers, and high-impact muckrakers.

As Theodore Hamm noted in his book on this period, *The New Blue Media: How Michael Moore, MoveOn.org, Jon Stewart and Company Are Transforming Progressive Politics*, "the New Blue Media have succeeded in transforming the style and, to a lesser extent, the substance of progressive politics."[8]

Maybe that's why the reelection of George W. Bush was a shock to so many.

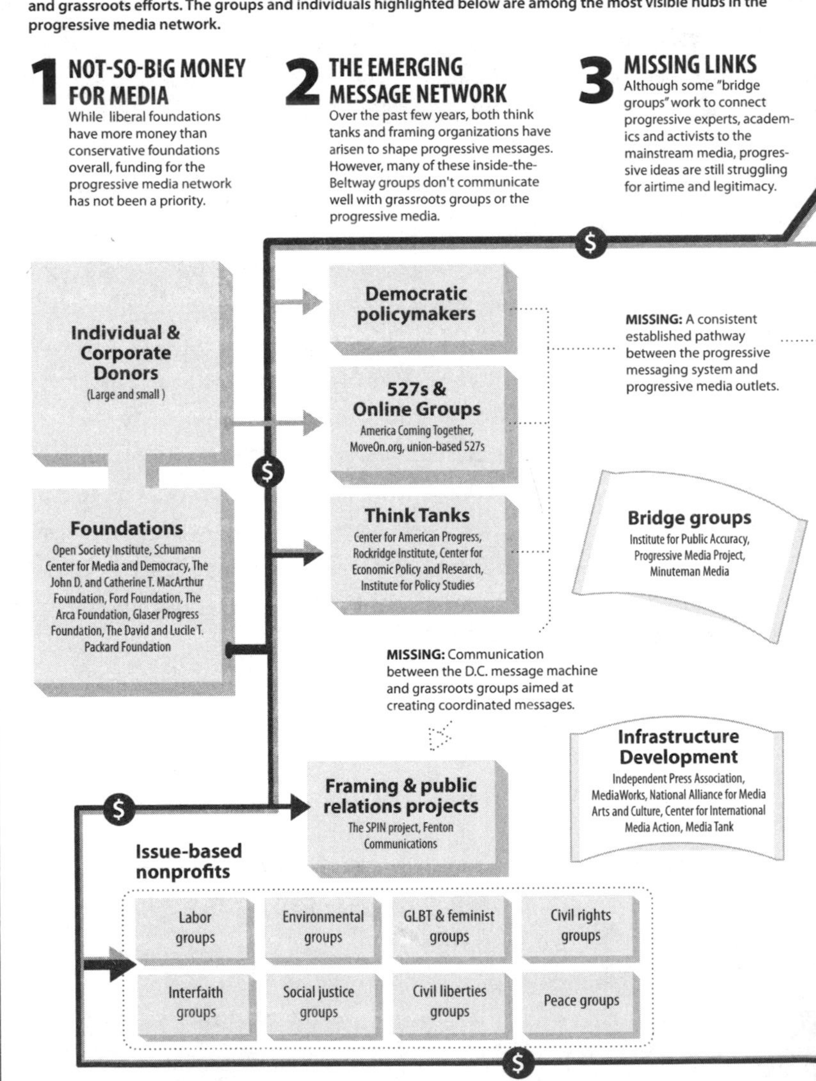

This 2005 map of the emerging progressive media network reflects the active debate about infrastructure that was taking place among activists and funders at the time. Produced by Tracy Van Slyke and Jessica Clark. Lead researcher:

The Emerging Progressive Media Network

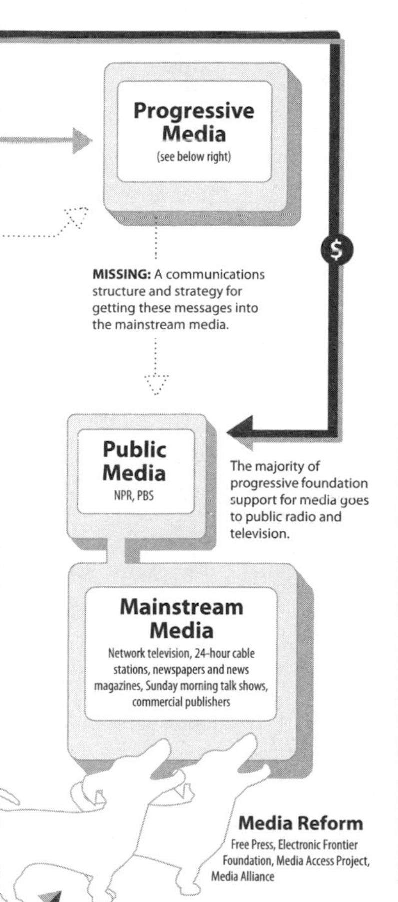

Key Differences

This table points out the structural and political differences between the conservative and progressive media sectors.

PROGRESSIVE MEDIA	CONSERVATIVE MEDIA
Ad hoc	Deliberately organized
Diverse and democractic	Top-down
Social justice agenda	Corporate agenda
Underfunded, difficult-to-sustain media projects	Successful for-profits and fully funded nonprofit media projects
Multiple messages	Coordinated messages
Struggling for coverage and legitimacy	Large-scale mainstream media impact

Progressive Media

Online magazines
AlterNet, TomPaine, Grist, Women's eNews, Pop and Politics

Online portals
Common Dreams, BuzzFlash, OneWorld.net, Institute for Global Communications

Independent community media
Alternative newsweeklies, public access cable TV, Low Power FM, Indy Media Centers

Publishers
Seven Stories Press, The New Press, Nation Books, Soft Skull Press

Magazines
The Nation, The American Prospect, Mother Jones, In These Times, The Progressive, plus many issue-based periodicals, like *ColorLines* & *Bitch*

Public intellectuals
Howard Zinn, Naomi Klein, Cornel West, Barbara Ehrenreich, Tom Frank, Laura Flanders, Norman Solomon, Noam Chomsky, among many others

Radio networks
Air America Radio, Democracy Radio, Pacifica, Free Speech Radio, nonprofit community radio stations

Satellite/cable/digital TV
Free Speech TV, Independent World Television (pending), many independent producers

Documentary producers
Robert Greenwald, Michael Moore, Shola Lynch

Journalists/pundits
Bill Moyers, Al Franken, Arianna Huffington, Michael Eric Dyson, Amy Goodman, Molly Ivins, Eric Alterman, Gloria Steinem, Jim Hightower

Blogs
Daily Kos, Eschaton, Talking Points Memo

Foundations and individual donors have started supporting media watchdog and policy reform organizations.

Pallav Vora. Additional research support: Laura Chomyn, Stephen Kovach, Anna Schneider, and Jennifer Wedekind. Design: Mikhaela Reid.

Jessica Clark and Tracy Van Slyke, "The Emerging Progressive Media Network," *In These Times*, May 9, 2005, http://www.inthesetimes.com/images/29/12/progressivemap.pdf

AFTER THE FALL

After November 2004, many progressive media makers felt that their work had had no impact on the outcome of the election or a general change in tone for the country, and were looking for explanations. For others, this was the proof that blogs and online communications tools were little more than a flash in the pan.

But whether they knew it or not, there was no going back now; the stage had been set for an explosion of online resources, journalism, and creativity. A growing number of audience members continued to flock to both existing and new progressive media sources. And while the infrastructure for an effective progressive media network was still in pieces, there were some who were looking not only at how to put the pieces together but also at what the final system would look like.

"After John Kerry's shattering defeat in the 2004 election, organizers, political leaders, pundits and funders all agreed that without a significant boost in progressive media capacity to provide a counter to the highly partisan right-wing media, the chances for liberal and progressive issues to gain traction and for Democrats to return to power, were questionable," wrote Don Hazen, the executive editor of AlterNet, in an April 2006 retrospective on the postelection period. AlterNet has long served as a hub for national progressive media, and Hazen was writing to celebrate "the newfound muscle in progressive media in the Bush era. The dynamics have changed. A fresh breed of smart, relentless media operatives, using the internet in creative ways, have put new pop into progressive media."[9]

For many progressives, 2005 was the dawn of a new era. Multiple external factors were challenging long-held assumptions and rules for progressive media's operations, communications, and interactions with the public. Plus, the Bush administration's legitimacy began to plummet in August 2005 after Hurricane Katrina demonstrated the administration's utter inability to handle domestic disasters.

Corruption scandals within the Republican party also started coming to light in Bush's second term (many times due to the efforts of the progressive media; more on that throughout the book). While mainstream media outlets were still slow on the uptake, the parade of scandals—including the treatment and detainment of foreign combatants at Guantánamo, campaign finance violation charges leveled against House Majority Leader Tom DeLay, lobbying irregularities by Capitol Hill insider and lobbyist Jack Abramoff, the aftermath of Hurricane Katrina, and the National Security Administration's illegal wiretapping of U.S. citizens—was difficult to ignore.

Cowed by persistent charges of liberal bias, weakened by ongoing consolidation of newspapers and radio and television outlets, and losing ad revenue and readers to online news sources, members of the commercial journalism establishment were facing their own internal crises. No one so eloquently skewered the spotty performance of the fourth estate as comedian Stephen Colbert at the April 2006 White House Correspondents Dinner:

> As excited as I am to be here with the president, I am appalled to be surrounded by the liberal media that is destroying America, with the exception of Fox News. Fox News gives you both sides of every story: the president's side, and the vice president's side.
>
> But the rest of you, what are you thinking, reporting on NSA wiretapping or secret prisons in eastern Europe? Those things are secret for a very important reason: they're super-depressing. And if that's your goal, well, misery accomplished.
>
> Over the last five years you people were so good—over tax cuts, WMD intelligence, the effect of global warming.

> We Americans didn't want to know, and you had the courtesy not to try to find out. Those were good times, as far as we knew.
>
> But, listen, let's review the rules. Here's how it works: the president makes decisions. He's the Decider. The press secretary announces those decisions, and you people of the press type those decisions down. Make, announce, type. Just put 'em through a spell check and go home. Get to know your family again. Make love to your wife. Write that novel you got kicking around in your head. You know, the one about the intrepid Washington reporter with the courage to stand up to the administration. You know—fiction![10]

The year 2005 also marked the explosion and wholesale emergence of Web 2.0 tools—blogs were only the beginning. The online video site YouTube launched in February 2005, powering a groundswell of both amateur videography and the repurposing of legacy content for commentary and satire. In April, investors pumped $2 million into Delicious, now a widely used social bookmarking site. Rupert Murdoch's News Corporation purchased MySpace in July, signaling the popular arrival of social networks. And Apple's October launch of the video iPod marked the rise of a new generation of more versatile multimedia mobile devices.

These political and technological shifts powered a watershed year for progressive media makers and outlets, allowing them to sharpen their individual roles within the larger sector, integrate new media opportunities for increased impact and reach, and construct a nascent infrastructure. By the following year, significant growth had occurred in the progressive media landscape.

When Democrats took control of both the House and Senate after the 2006 elections, this served as a proving ground for both the blogosphere and a newly empowered set of progressive pundits, analysts, and outlets, with pitched media battles around progressive candidates such as Ned Lamont, who challenged Senator

WEB 2.0 MEDIA TRENDS INCLUDE:

- More free content, available 24/7
- New tools for tagging, ranking, and sharing print/audio/video content
- An increased emphasis on search engines as primary interfaces, as users attempt to navigate an overwhelming flood of news and information
- The rise of video sharing and video conversation, via platforms like YouTube, Blip.tv, and Seesmic
- Widespread availability of streaming audio and podcasts
- The rise of both large-scale and targeted social networks
- Routine copying, sharing, and remixing of media content
- New mobile platforms: the iPhone and beyond
- RSS feeds, newsreaders, SMS, and more

These have led to new roles for media consumers:

- Finding content
- Ranking content
- Tagging content
- Creating content
- Distributing content
- Mocking content

Joe Lieberman (I-Conn.), and hot-button issues such as government wiretapping. In some cases, progressive bloggers and journalists struggled to keep up with developments in media spheres they were less familiar with, around issues such as immigration.

The Emerging Progr

THE EMERGING NETWORK

Over the past year, media organizations and outlets have begun to work with newsmakers to move progressive issues and narratives into the national debate. New technologies and distribution methods are also expanding the progressive media audience.

1 MAKING THE NEWS

Agenda setters in the beltway and progressive organizations generate action, media alerts and research to drive the news cycle.

Ne

Progressive Base

Democratic Voters

Activist Audience

Mass Audience

4 THE RISING POLITICAL MEDI

Infrastructure-building e
focus on making indepe
progressive media more
and expanding its audie

5 GAPS IN THE SYSTEM

The pipelines for funneling progressive ideas, experts and narratives into the mainstream media need to be developed further.

Mainstream Commercial Media

Network and cable TV, radio networks, online and print magazines, newspapers, book publishers, film and entertainment companies

Public Niche M

Public TV and radi
ethnic media, n
TV proj

This 2006 map shows both the increasing strength of the progressive media network and the rising power of active, networked users.

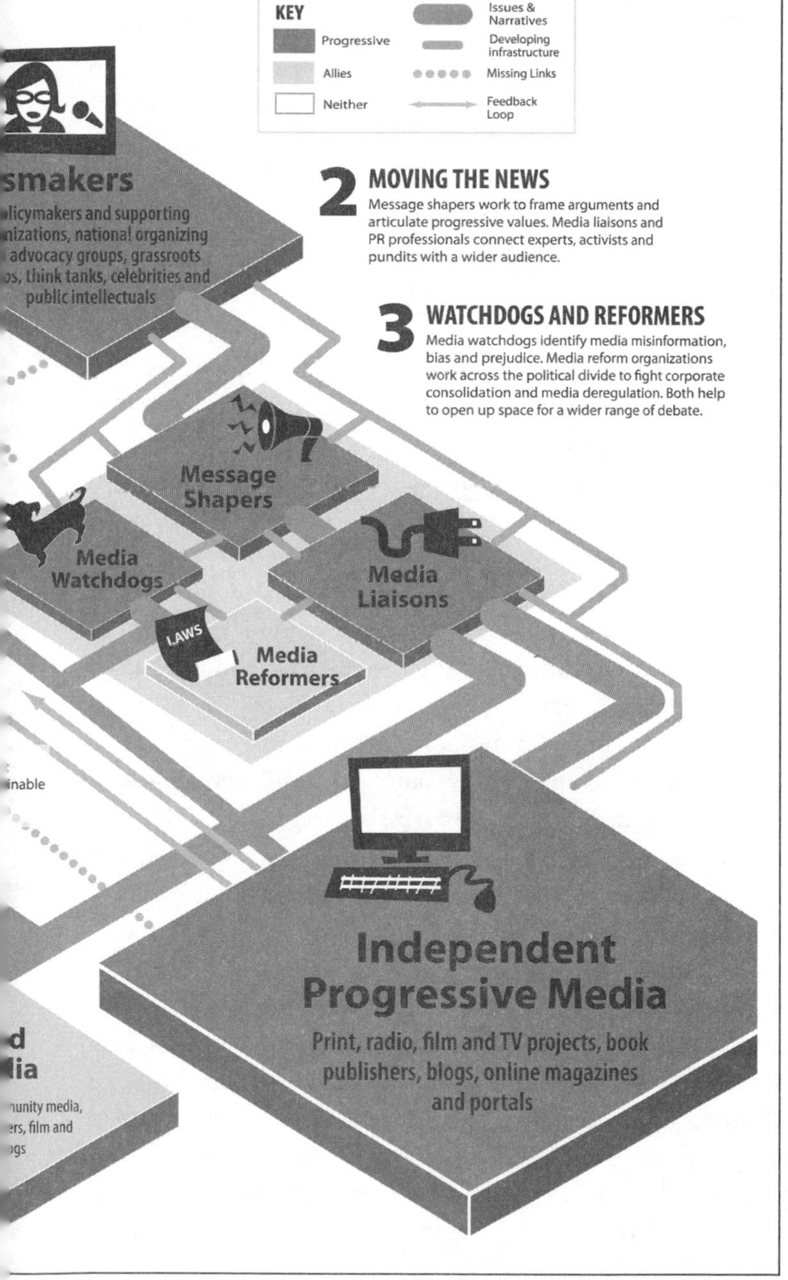

Jessica Clark and Tracy Van Slyke, "The Emerging Progressive Media Network 2006," *In These Times*, July 2006, http://www.inthesetimes.com/multimedia/mediamap/

In 2006, more than a million immigrants and allies took over the streets of Los Angeles, Chicago, Washington, D.C., and many cities in between. These protests, the largest the country had seen since the start of the Iraq war, were largely powered by a combination of advocacy work, text messaging, social networking, and Spanish-language radio.

The new tools were also offering new opportunities and spaces for a variety of organizers and media makers who traditionally had been shut out of both mainstream and traditional left outlets—including feminists, GLBTQQ (gay, lesbian, bisexual, transgender, queer, and questioning) activists, ethnic media makers, and youth. While grassroots anarchist and antiglobalization activists had been pioneers in participatory online organizing and publishing, largely through the network of Independent Media Center sites, they were not always on the inside of the new Beltway-focused progressive discussions. But they continued to foster their own networks and outlets, overlapping occasionally on trade or other issues. Meanwhile, conservatives were not quick to adapt to the social media environment, giving progressives and their allies an early-adopter advantage.

But just as a revamped progressive media sector began to gel, the proliferation of Web 2.0 tools and platforms threatened to overtake the influence of legacy progressive magazines. While the audiences for progressive content were increasing across the board, new pundits, voices, and platforms drew progressive readers away from the old standbys, which relied on a top-down mode of communication that was often less engaging and/or entertaining.

More and more, audience members were no longer passive consumers but active participants in the creation and dissemination of media. The launch of the iPhone in January 2007 offered new horizons for mobile media. As traditional outlets struggled to survive, power blogs such as Daily Kos and the Huffington Post were thriving, bolstered by low staff costs and the free content provided by their own audience members. And now the threat of obsolescence extended beyond print media to the blogosphere, which was succeeded by a "vlogosphere," featuring amateur videos; a "podosphere," featuring audio productions; and on into the "tweetosphere," which featured bite-sized bursts of text that users could submit via cell phones and online to Twitter. Platforms such as Mogulus and new tools such as Qik gave users the power to report and broadcast live television online. Just like those in the commercial media spheres, progressive media makers scrambled to learn and adjust.

All of these technological and political advancements were hastened by the new connections users could now make with one another. A yet more decentralized online media system was rising, driven largely by user recommendation, referrals from search engines, and linked content. Facebook opened its doors to all users in 2006, driving a surge in social networking by those past college age, and inspiring a wave of related online start-ups. The "Social Media Starfish," below—a graphic designed by writer and marketer Darren Barefoot in response to a video by Scobelizer blogger Robert Scoble—suggests the rapid proliferation of social media platforms in this period.

All of these changes have contributed to shifting media consumption habits and opinions. In a February 2008 Zogby poll,[11] 48 percent of the respondents said their primary source of news and information was the Internet, an 8 percent increase from the previous year. And the notion of what constitutes credible journalism is changing: 67 percent of the respondents said that they thought traditional journalism was out of touch. At the same time, 87 percent of the total respondents believe professional journalism has a vital role to play in journalism's future, although "citizen journalism" (77 percent) and blogging (59 percent) were also seen as significant.

Social networks, new video platforms, and citizen media all played a major role in the 2008 election cycle, foiling conservative efforts to control the story line and spread smears, and breath-

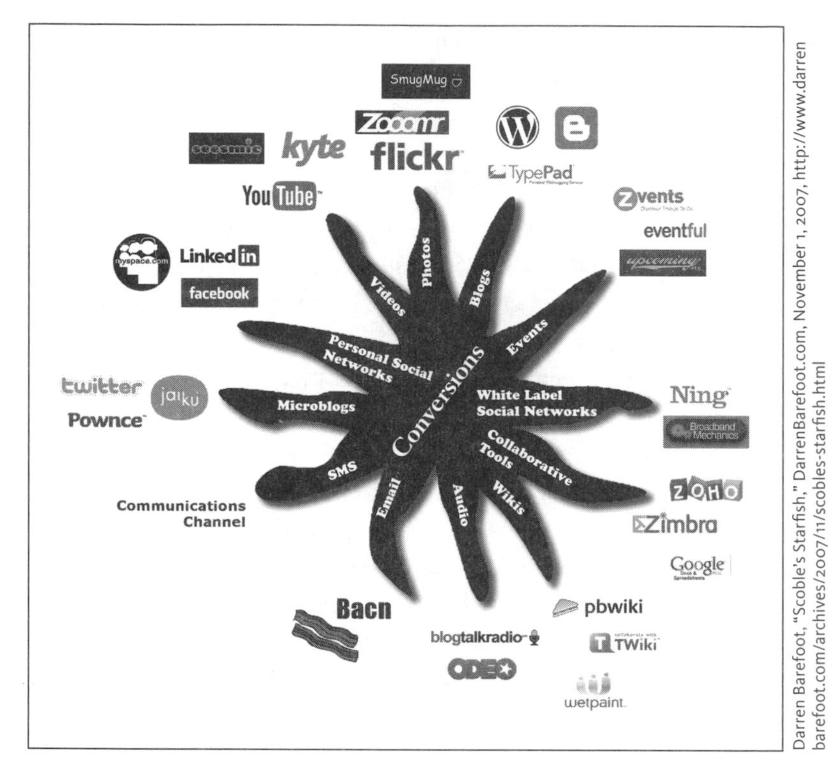

The Social Media Starfish demonstrates the many different kinds of social network platforms that had sprung up by 2008.

Darren Barefoot, "Scoble's Starfish," DarrenBarefoot.com, November 1, 2007, http://www.darren barefoot.com/archives/2007/11/scobles-starfish.html

ing new life into organizing efforts. Presidential debates hosted by MTV and CNN took on a new character as online contributors were invited to submit questions live or via YouTube. Despite howls of media bias from the right, progressive news and blog sites such as the Huffington Post gained readers and legitimacy—by October 2008, according to Nielsen Online, the site's traffic had jumped an eye-popping 448 percent from the previous October.[12] The campaigns themselves spent unprecedented time and money on social and mobile media, especially the Obama campaign, which worked with a Facebook founder to create its own customized social network, MyBarackObama.com.

As the *New York Times* put it in a November 2, 2008 article:

> For many viewers, the 2008 election has become a kind of hybrid in which the dividing line between online and off, broadcast and cable, pop culture and civic culture, has been all but obliterated.
>
> Many of the media outlets influencing the 2008 election simply were not around in 2004. YouTube did not exist, and Facebook barely reached beyond the Ivy League. There was no Huffington Post to encourage citizen reporters, so Mr. Obama's comment about voters clinging to guns or religion may have passed unnoticed. These sites and countless others have redefined how many Americans get their political news.[13]

One such redefinition was the rise of MSNBC as an increasingly secure home for progressive reporters and commentators. Previous efforts to establish a left-leaning counterpoint to Fox News on cable had failed, as Jeff Cohen, founder of the media watchdog group Fairness and Accuracy in Reporting (FAIR), recounted in his 2006 book, *Cable News Confidential: My Misadventures in Corporate Media*. While Cohen detailed the abortive attempt to launch a progressive prime-time show hosted by Phil Donahue in the early years of the Bush administration, Keith Olbermann, the host of MSNBC's *Countdown*, had more luck. In February 2006, the bombastic host—given to delivering high-toned "special comments" lambasting the administration and other bad actors—began signing off each night with a countdown of the number of days since Bush's declaration of "mission accomplished."

Olbermann's aggressive and humorous competition with Fox News star Bill O'Reilly dovetailed with *The Colbert Report*'s satirical worship of O'Reilly as "Papa Bear," starting in October 2005. This double-barreled assault marked the widespread acknowledgment that conservatives had been shamelessly dominating the airwaves. The popularity of *Countdown* allowed MSNBC to launch another overtly progressive program in August 2008: *The Rachel Maddow Show*, which had already doubled the audience for its time slot just a month after its launch, and has served as a platform for a range of progressive journalists and commentators.

By the end of 2008's long and contested presidential campaign, the Republican Noise Machine seemed to be running out of steam, reflecting the crumbling of its political and ideological apparatus as well. Repeated efforts to launch swiftboating campaigns against the Obama campaign had fallen flat with all but the most dedicated red-state partisans. In a November 5 article on the progressive news portal Common Dreams, Cohen wrote:

> The media terrain has changed dramatically since 2004 when Matt Drudge dominated the Net with his anti-Kerry vendetta. Today Huffington Post—which didn't even launch until 2005—gets more visitors than Drudge. While conservative and establishment pundits still dominate TV and radio, progressive dominance of the Internet has made it easier for media critics and bloggers to instantly rebut the kind of hoaxes and smears that so damaged Gore and Kerry.
>
> This time Swift-Boating was often countered—as when Obama refused to be eclipsed by TV clips of Rev. Wright and made his speech on race that became the top video on You Tube (1.5 million views, 4,000 comments in 36 hours.) With Wright a media obsession, indy journalists from Glenn Greenwald to David Corn exposed McCain's bigoted preacher/endorsers.
>
> Years ago, rightwing smears would flow up the food chain from Drudge to Fox News/talk radio into mainstream media. This year, the flow of serious, accurate charges about McCain got a push from progressive media—like the story of "McCain's Mansions," which sailed from blogs to mainstream via the hugely successful Brave New Films viral video.

> Few will forget McCain's stunning answer when asked how many homes he owned: "I think—I'll have my staff get to you."[14]

Cohen's description reveals the evolution of the progressive media sector, now faced with a new task: holding a Democrat accountable instead of just playing opposition. In order to make an impact in the participatory media environment, progressive media outlets would need to move into a new mode of operation: network-powered media. How would they define impact beyond the echo chamber?

The next two chapters examine the dynamics of network-powered progressive media, and the evolution of new forms of impact measurement. Section II offers a grounded overview of six strategies that progressive media makers have used to spark social and political change. And in Section III, we offer recommendations for the future.

A SHORT LIST OF PROGRESSIVE MEDIA OUTLETS, 2009

BY JESSICA CLARK AND TRACY VAN SLYKE

National Political Blogs
Crooks and Liars
Daily Kos
Eschaton
Firedoglake
Glenn Greenwald (*Salon*)
Hullabaloo
Majikthise
MyDD
OpenLeft
Think Progress

See the full list at leftyblogs.com

"Afrosphere" (African American Blogosphere)
Afro-Netizen
Black Agenda Report
Jack and Jill Politics
Pam's House Blend (also LGBT)

Hispanic National Blogosphere
The Sanctuary
The Unapologetic Mexican

Feminist National Blogosphere
Broadsheet (*Salon*)
Feministe
Feministing
Pandagon
Racialicious

See the selected list at http://linkfluence.net/feminism20

State Blogs and News Sites
Democracy for New Mexico
Michigan Liberal
Progress Illinois
WriteWhatSheLikes (Ohio)

Book Publishers
Berrett-Koehler
Chelsea Green
Haymarket Books
Monthly Review Press
The New Press
Seal Press
Seven Stories
South End Press

Magazines
ColorLines
Hightower Lowdown
In These Times
Mother Jones
Ms. Magazine
Sojourners
The American Prospect
The Nation
The Progressive
The Texas Observer
The Washington Monthly
Utne Reader

Online News Sites (original content)
Grist
RH Reality Check
Salon
Talking Points Memo
The Washington Independent

Online Video News
The Real News Network
Brave New Films
The Uptake

Online News Aggregators (original and reprinted content)
AlterNet
BuzzFlash
Common Dreams
Huffington Post
Media Channel
New America Media
The Raw Story
TruthDig
One World

Radio Networks
Air America
Pacifica
Public News Service

Individual Radio Shows
Democracy Now!
Free Speech Radio News
Making Contact
RadioNation

Television Networks
Free Speech TV
Link TV

Individual Television Projects
GRITtv (online and Free Speech TV)
The Rachel Maddow Show (MSNBC)
The Young Turks (online)

2
NETWORKING YOUR WAY TO IMPACT

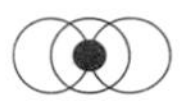

To understand strategies for successful impact, it is key to understand the new landscape we are operating within. In fact, many progressive outlets helped to shape this new landscape, while others stepped in to take full strategic advantage. And of course there were and continue to be those still struggling to navigate this environment.

We have identified four layers of networks that progressive media outlets must strategically integrate into their planning to shape and distribute coverage for maximum impact:

- Networked users
- Self-organized networks
- Institutional networks
- Networks of institutions

Below we outline the implications and opportunities that come from these networks.

NETWORKED USERS

Tens of millions of individuals are engaging with the networked public sphere, using online tools and platforms to find, rank, tag, create, distribute, mock, and recommend content (as described in Chapter 1). For the sake of simplicity, we are calling them "users"—a combination of audience member and participant.

Observers of media and politics are coming up with various terms for these proactive, connected types, many of whom belong to the so-called Millennial Generation. In a report for the Case Foundation, Demos senior fellow Allison Fine calls them "Social Citizens, representing a nascent model and era of citizen participation that combines idealism, digital fluency, and immersion in social causes."[1] Part of the biggest generation since the baby boom, Social Citizens are more mobile, more global, more socially conscious, and more wired than generations born before 1978, writes Fine.

Millennials aren't the whole story, though—a January 2009 report from the Pew Internet and American Life Project breaks down the generations according to Internet usage.[2] As of late 2008, this study suggests, older generations of users were catching up, with the largest increase in Internet use since 2005 in the seventy- to seventy-five-year-old age group. E-mail was more popular as a communication tool among older users, while teens and Millennials were more likely to use social networking sites, instant messaging, and personal blogs to communicate with friends. They were also more likely to use the Web for entertainment: playing games, participating in virtual worlds, and watching online video.

The advent of simple online tools and platforms for publishing photos, audio, and video has dramatically shifted the ability of individuals to create political media. YouTube was first recognized by the establishment as not only a cultural force but a political one in August 2006 when Senator George Allen (R-Va.) was caught on video at a public rally referring to an aide of his opponent Jim Webb with the derogatory slur "Macaca."[3] Hundreds of thousands watched the video on YouTube, propelling it to progressive and establishment media coverage; it eventually torpedoed Allen's reelection and ultimate presidential bid. PoliticsTV, a progressive online TV channel, named the Macaca video the "number one political video of all time" in March 2007.[4]

In 2008, hundreds of progressive political and advocacy groups—along with thousands of individuals—turned to short-form video to advocate for their favored political candidate or issue. As *The Nation*'s Ari Melber reported on November 4, 2008, "Out of the top twenty videos focusing on Obama, only one was produced by his campaign, an advertisement contrasting his economic credentials with John McCain's. Three other Obama videos came from McCain's headquarters, as viewers flocked to see sensational attack ads slamming the Democratic nominee as the latest celebrity. Most of the top videos, however, were created by ordinary people who were simply excited about politics or pop culture."[5]

The surge in Web 2.0 opens up pathways for progressive media to create unprecedented forms of outreach and more intimate engagement with current audiences. The audience has morphed into users who are connected to both the outlet and multiple social networks. They can take on a myriad of roles that benefit the outlet. Ultimately, such interactions empower users with information and activities that can increase the impact of the news and information being disseminated.

Many individuals use media content as the basis for activism. These are the users who go beyond just news consumption to using the news as a force for mobilization. They can do things as simple as send a story or clip through e-mail, post it on Facebook, or recommend it on shared sites such as Reddit or Digg. They can also move into more activist roles offered on the sites of blogs or media outlets: signing petitions, joining actions, donating money, attending events, and much more (as described in Chapter 8: "Assemble the Progressive Choir").

When asked how their audiences use their content in a late 2008 survey co-produced by our respective organizations, progressive media outlets responded with some direct examples.

ColorLines, a magazine on race and politics published by the Applied Research Center, sent us a quote from one reader who responded to an article about postracialism in an Obama presidential era. "This is an absolutely crucial educational moment about how very UNpostrace this country is, and I hope everyone who reads this and other ARC online pieces will email them to as many contacts as possible. . . . Say it loud and say it proud: We are racial justice activists whose time has COME, not gone."

Democracy Now!, one of the most popular progressive daily radio news programs in the country, told us that they receive tons of responses from listeners and fans similar to this one: "I wanted to say how thankful and grateful I am that I was able to have the opportunity to hear Amy [Goodman] speak. . . . Never before have I been so inspired to participate. Already I have begun to become a lot more active in speaking out against the war."

Progressive media users can also become emissaries for an outlet's brand. As traditional marketing techniques and advertising lose their influence and the information glut becomes difficult to sift through, validation from peers about good and necessary content becomes one of the key ways that new users find information.

A viewer of Link TV, a national channel focusing on global perspectives and news, wrote to the channel with this message: "I just wanted to express my gratitude to you for all the rich information that you provide me every day. Because of you I have learned a lot about the world, I have opened my mind, and I have met many incredible people who have inspired me to read more, listen more and judge less. I have become a Link TV addict and I promise to keep watching, spread the word and keep my donations up too."

An experimental area for progressive media organizations is integrating users directly into content production. Media organizations have had different reactions as users become more proactive, comfortable, and sophisticated in creating their own content as well as analyzing content from other sources. Some journalism organizations panic as they imagine that their "expert" role will all but disappear. Others look at it as an opportunity to build a different kind of news organization focused only on work from "citizen journalists" (as described in Chapter 6, "Embrace Twenty-First-Century Muckraking").

We believe that there can be a strategic balance between the two, and that's what progressive media makers must strive for over the next few years. There will still be a vital role for those trained in journalism with specific areas of expertise, especially as the corporate media continue to crumble. There's also a role for the citizen journalist, as more and more become trained in the art of reporting and production.

For example, The UpTake, an online video news organization serviced by a small group of staff and a large group of citizen journalists, reported that their ongoing coverage of the 2008 Republican National Convention (RNC) proved their model of collaborative journalism. The UpTake's citizen journalist crews were on the scene as local and federal police raided homes and arrested hundreds of peaceful protestors and even arrested dozens of professional journalists. No one from the corporate media was there to cover those stories, nor reported on it later.

"During the five days of the RNC, our team of many dozens of citizen journalists produced more than 160 videos," said The UpTake. More than one million people viewed the videos. Many of the users then acted as emissaries, sending the video content around to their networks of peers, colleagues, and families. (We know we did.) Many more examples of citizen media production are examined in "Embrace Twenty-First-Century Muckraking."

In an interview for a Media Consortium strategic planning project in 2008, Clay Shirky, author of *Here Comes Everybody: The Power of Organizing without Organizing* and a professor at New York University's graduate Interactive Telecommunications Program, said, "The thing to realize is [for these models] it's not just enough to have a place where readers talk back—or the classic 'letters to the editors' pattern. Rather it's about providing a platform for readers to coordinate with one another. That's a really radical shift because in part it means you have to take community seriously. The word 'membership' has a nice feeling, but what media outlets usually mean by this is: give me money and we'll give a product or access. But real membership is about coming together on shared projects, and this is extremely rare. The convening power of media organizations is a power they haven't used because of their model, but the potential is huge."[6]

Progressive media outlets must continue to increase their conversations and connections with connected individual users, whether they're bringing users creatively into the distribution process, allowing users to advocate for the media outlet to their peers, or inviting users to strategically partake in the editorial planning and content creation process.

SELF-ORGANIZED NETWORKS

As the online space transforms, users also are moving away from more informal activist and emissary roles to forming self-organized groups that use content—produced by both individuals and progressive media makers—to inform and navigate political and social debates, policy battles, and events. These self-organized networks form the next layer that media makers should integrate into their editorial and business strategies.

Networked individual users tend to be part of many overlapping online groups, crossing boundaries of work, play, and politics. Such groups can be fleeting or durable, open or closed, sprawling or focused—but each offers media makers the possibility of amplifying issues, engaging in viral outreach, and attracting new supporters and users.

A February 2009 post by MIT media scholar Henry Jenkins reviews a variety of terms for connected users of media—"prosumers," "influencers," or, as New York University journalism professor Jay Rosen has called them, "people formerly known as the audience"—and the networks they inhabit. Jenkins notes that networks can be organized around common endeavors (pools), around individual social connections (webs), or around a brand or celebrity (hubs). Whatever the structure, Jenkins suggests, the rise of networks has precipitated a shift for media makers—from creating "sticky" content that keeps users' attention to making "spreadable" content that prompts them to share and act. He writes:

> Most brands will need to court a range of different communities and travel across pools, webs, and hubs if they want to reach the full range of desired consumers. To achieve that, they must embrace what filmmaker Lance Weiler calls "The Scattershot Approach." The idea is to be available for your users in whichever way and every way they deem appropriate, be it through a web site, widget, RSS feed or embeddable video, making the process of finding and communicating with you as easy and enjoyable as possible.[7]

While Jenkins is describing these processes for commercial brands, progressive media makers can also take advantage of the power of networks. They can seek to turn their own outlets into pools or hubs, through conversation boards, live chats, and other social media tools. They can tap into existing webs of users, including those organized on Facebook or Twitter. And they can train their editors and reporters to tap their own networks in order to start highly focused conversations around stories and issues.

Shifting from a top-down, report-and-broadcast model to a multiplatform conversational mode can feel like a sacrifice. For traditional journalists, reaching out to networked individuals once again seems like a loss of control. But at this point, let's be honest: who's got control anyway? To stay relevant, media outlets need to rethink their core functions and shift from just producing content to building communities that join and foster online conversations whenever they can. These media spaces will have to provide the technology, context, and spaces for short- and long-term networks to self-organize, allowing users to debate, create, take action, and disseminate media around their shared interests.

The "Value Maps" produced by the organizers of the Journalism That Matters community of journalists, academics, media entrepreneurs, and more (see p. 41) demonstrate the new roles for users, journalists, and outlets in the "emerging news ecology."

In another interview with The Media Consortium in 2008, Amy Gahran, media consultant and blogger for the Poynter Institute's E-Media Tidbits, said, "We're getting away from the idea that a journalist tells a story—it will be that a journalist offers a window for people to create their own meaning."

She continued, "When you have a packaged news story—it puts it into this story with all this narrative and then it presents the information and then it is done. It doesn't give people room to say, 'What are the other stories?' or 'That stat is interesting, but what does that mean for me?' It leaves them helpless with what to do with the information."[8]

In addition to creating the spaces on their sites for self-organized networks to form and take action, media organizations will also actively have to pursue networks where they already exist. They are going to have to go where the users are, not wait for users to find them. There are thousands of Facebook groups, blogs, Twitter feeds, listservs, and more where self-organized groups virtually gather. Media outlets will have to figure out how to authentically interact with these groups, using the real voices of their writers, editors, producers, and contributors. Last but not least, they will have to use this interaction to bring some of those users back into their Web sites and integrate them into those community spaces.

It's important to note that self-organizing networks won't always operate the way you might expect. A January 16, 2009, post in the *New York Times* online illustrates this point, describing how a group of activists flooded Barack Obama's transition site, Change.gov, asking whether the Obama administration "would appoint a

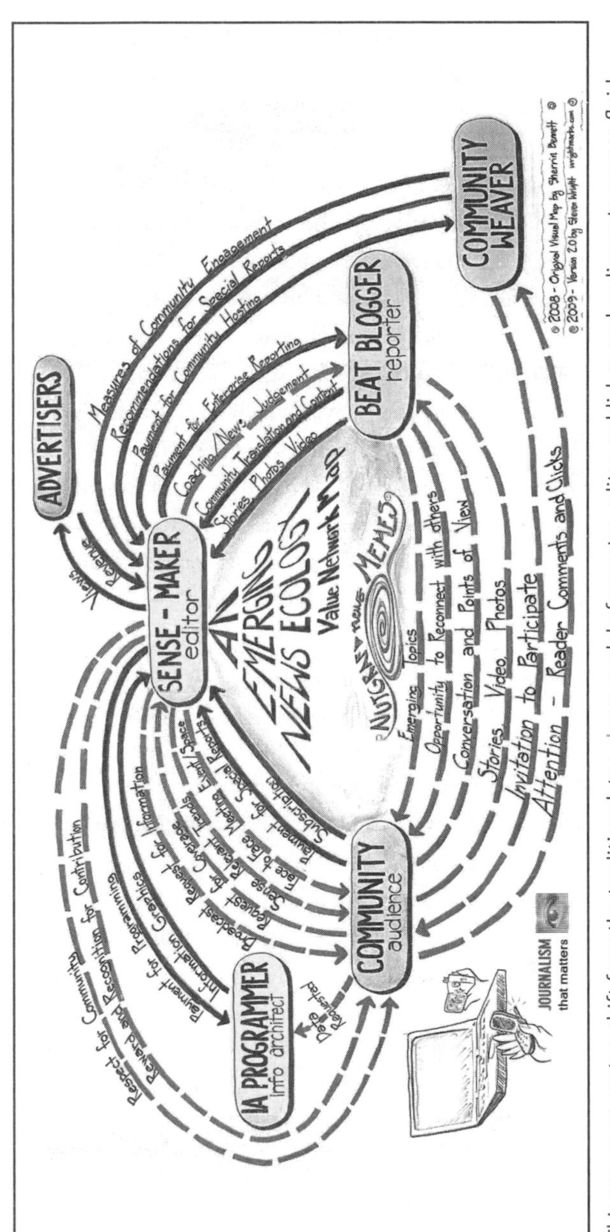

Sherrin Bennett, "Value Network Maps," Journalism That Matters, February 25, 2009, http://journalismthatmatters.com/content/value-network-maps

This map represents a shift from the traditional, top-down model of reporter, editor, publisher, and audience to a more fluid ecosystem in which "beat bloggers" relate horizontally to community members in conversations about topics, stories, photos, and chances to participate. In this model, the editor serves as a sort of traffic cop, routing payments and assignments to the "beat blogger," requests for feedback to the user community, and assignments to programmers that help to create and enrich the community environment. A "community weaver" serves as a check on the system, hosting the community, assessing the impact of stories and conversations, and offering suggestions for hot topics to cover more deeply.

special prosecutor to investigate possible Bush Administration war crimes." Melber of *The Nation* (he's one networked user!) described the results.

> It is striking that Obama's aides, who helped win the election by harnessing new media, believed they could just spin away from their online interlocutors. Instead, the move backfired immediately. Bob Fertik, the activist who submitted the question, campaigned for it; and progressive websites, including thenation.com, blasted the dodge. Within a day, MSNBC's Keith Olbermann picked up the story. A day later, Obama was compelled to answer the question in an interview with ABC's George Stephanopoulos, who quoted it and pressed Obama with two follow-ups. Obama's answer, which prioritized moving "forward" but did not rule out a special prosecutor, made the front page of the January 12 *New York Times*.[9]

User uprisings such as this one are common to social networks. But by keeping an open flow of communication, a transparent record of interactions, and a sense of humor, media makers can learn to harness and benefit even from dissent. For outlets that embrace communication with networks of users, the paybacks are manifold: an increase in feedback loops that can inform deeper coverage, increased loyalty, access to new and targeted audiences, and more buzz. All of these result in greater impact, more influence, and more resources.

Self-organizing networks can also serve to strengthen traditional journalistic practice. In a March 17, 2009, article, *Politico* political media reporter Michael Calderone broke the story of a listserv populated by both progressive and more establishment reporters. Called JournoList, this discussion group was started by the *American Prospect*'s Ezra Klein in early 2007 and by 2009 had more than three hundred members (including us). The problem with the story was visible in its online headline: "JournoList: Inside the Echo Chamber." The false notion here was that because they gathered together in one virtual "coffeehouse," these journalists were conspiring to write in lockstep in an echo chamber model. Despite the salacious headline, nothing in the article documented evidence of an echo chamber effect. What it did show was that some reporters are no longer working in isolation or even in competition but are actively learning from and sharing with each other—along with arguing with each other, which can only help the vibrancy and depth of their work.

NETWORKS ORGANIZED BY INSTITUTIONS

In contrast to the organic networks organized by individuals, there are a number of more focused networks that institutions have purposely developed in order to mobilize users to action around key issues. From the Sierra Club to the American Civil Liberties Union (ACLU) to the National Organization for Women (NOW), many membership-based advocacy organizations are working to transition from a broadcast communication model to a networked mode in order to interact with their members. Some, such as MoveOn and Color of Change, are Web-native organizations that have pioneered new ways of reaching members online and moving them to action. We also include in this category influential individuals who have created their own brand, active following, and business model (however small or large).

What does this mean for progressive media? The more activist progressive outlets have sometimes formed informal alliances with such organizations in the past, both reporting on their activities and partnering up to report on and advocate for related issues. (They have also been the target of such groups' organized letter-writing campaigns when they get the story wrong.) For the most part, however, journalists have shied away from direct organizing in partnership with institutional networks, fearing that they could be perceived as less than objective.

In the networked era, however, those relationships have the potential to become much more fluid. There are new opportunities to work with nonprofit and advocacy groups and the networks they command—for crowd-sourced reporting, story dissemination, or branding and fund-raising. Multiplatform content production offers many instances in which focused user networks can be engaged as stories move from print to audio to video and back again.

The key for progressive media working with networks organized by institutions is the type of relationship that is built. There are a series of questions to ask.

- How does your content relate to the network users' interests, goals, and issues?
- Will associating your outlet with an institution affect your credibility?
- Is there a chance to build your brand, create a durable audience?
- Most important, can this kind of partnership directly inform the eternal question of what people are doing because of the work you produced?

Through short and long-term partnerships, outlets can work with allies to funnel their content to institutional networks and directly track how this content is being used for action. Connecting content to outcomes is a critical component of demonstrating the impact of the progressive media. If done correctly, partnering with institutional networks helps make that connection clear.

NETWORKS OF INSTITUTIONS

Advocacy organizations, media outlets, community organizations, and more are also using social networking tools to connect with one another to share strategies and amplify impact. A number of off-the-record listservs, standing conference calls, and weekly meetings now serve to connect progressive nonprofits and advocacy groups with bloggers and journalists. Staying in such regular contact allows institutions to react quickly to news and policy cycles and maintain strategic connections between annual conferences. Such gatherings build upon the lessons of the infamous Wednesday meetings organized by high-profile conservative strategist Grover Norquist, which *USA Today* once called "the political equivalent of one-stop shopping." [10]

But while Norquist's goal was to unify talking points and political agendas for conservatives, progressive journalists generally refuse to coordinate with institutions to serve up lockstep talking points. And while journalistic institutions are forming networks to share tools and business strategies (as we document in Chapter 4, "Build Network-Powered Media"), even the bloggers have largely abandoned the idea of speaking with one voice. Here's Matt Stoller from mid-2007: "I guess sometimes unity makes sense from a strategic standpoint, but the lockstep idea is a bit silly. Boingboing, Grist, and DailyKos are very different places, yet it's possible to situate all of them under this big tent. If there is a core philosophy to what I call the 'Open Left,' it's a respect for pluralism, openness and participation. We like to hash things out. And hashing things out tends to create a sense of community and natural discipline, since you kind of figure out where the obvious areas of agreement are and move in that direction." [11]

So where does more direct coordination come into play? Bloggers and legacy media outlets can and should coordinate around shared reporting on complex issues, work together to build upon each other's strengths, and fill in each other's gaps. For example, a magazine might work with a video or television partner to use different platforms for producing journalism and cross-pollinating each other's audiences. Or a documentarian might offer online outtakes to a Web-only outlet in order to both promote the film and illuminate an issue.

Similarly, progressive outlets can strategically coordinate with advocacy organizations, think tanks, and grassroots organizations to drive traffic and awareness via single stories or shared long-term interest in a particular topic. As such networks of institutions develop, the partner institutions can cross-post reporting, devise action opportunities, jointly fund-raise, and more. Institutional networks can quickly snap together related networks of users, building momentum and impact around an issue, a piece of legislation, or an event. Collaborating behind the scenes to create joint models for revenue generation or joint investments in new technological platforms can also help to strengthen the progressive sector. Such alliances simultaneously build infrastructure and help individual partners adapt and remain relevant in a continuously changing media and political environment. The Media Consortium, a network of progressive journalism organizations, formed in early 2005 to strategically identify new ways to coordinate that would build the impact of their reporting on the political dialogue as well as find new ways to strengthen the overall infrastructure and sustainability of the sector. There's more on that organization in Chapter 4, "Build Network-Powered Media."

As institutions create their own networks, they will find new opportunities to join forces on critical issues, nimbly respond, and proactively influence the news cycle.

PULLING IT ALL TOGETHER

Once progressive media makers learn to recognize and navigate these different network layers, how can they leverage them for impact? Where do they fit into the maturing progressive infrastructure?

In the past, that would have depended mainly on how the organization defined itself: as a journalism-focused project that reports, investigates, and analyzes, or as a more activist-oriented project that strategizes with allies about campaigns and integrates different user and institutional networks around content?

Not anymore. The roles now shift and blur, and will continue to. Over the last four years, we have seen the rise of the blogosphere, powered by thousands of individuals who have become the online organizers and voices of millions of progressives. The legacy media outlets, rather than disappearing into oblivion, have put their stake in the ground, working to slowly develop an infrastructure that will move them into the future. And last but not least, *you* have taken the reins to redefine and re-create how journalism is conceptualized, created, and distributed.

All of this occurs in an ecosystem built upon connection and collaboration via multiple network layers.

To make an impact in this new media landscape, media outlets are going to have to become hybrids: publishers, listeners, reporters, opinors, co-creators, community builders, and more. They are also going to have to determine how they add the most value in order to break through the overwhelming chatter of our 24/7, worldwide connected media system.

3
WHY—AND HOW—PROGRESSIVE MEDIA MATTER

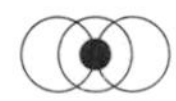

Measuring the success of progressive media projects has always been a complex matter. Independent media makers have had to stuff themselves into an ill-fitting model of commercial metrics: eyeballs and profits. These metrics often serve as the baseline for what marks a media organization as relevant and politically powerful. Such success didn't mean the media outlet provided quality reporting, mind you, only that it was effective in getting its reporting out to the world.

Progressive media have a different baseline for success—it's not just how much revenue they generate or how many people they reach, but how they alter the political discourse. While the new, networked media environment allows progressive media to have more impact, the tension remains. How do outlets and media makers break free from the corporate metrics and create a new paradigm for defining and describing the critical role of their organizations? What strategies can progressives use to make and support media that matters?

To redefine impact, we need to take another look at the relationship between mission and value. Stock price has become a primary indicator of value for many newspapers, for instance, with the mission of pleasing shareholders overpowering their civic mission.

What happens when you flip the equation, placing equal value on the social and political outcomes of media projects? Can we create a "double bottom line"—as environmentalists have done for sustainable products—that accounts for both profit and progressive change?

"Social movement journalism seeks to promote ideas, not profits; movement journals seek to challenge corporate control of media, not justify it," writes Bob Ostertag in *People's Movements, People's Press: The Journalism of Social Justice Movements*. "They address readers as members of communities, not individual consumers. They cover social movements as participants, not 'observers.' They exist to make change, not business. If the political context of a given movement at a particular time offers conditions in which a long-lived, large-circulation, profit-making journal can be strategically employed to further movement goals, then these are meaningful accomplishments. If such conditions are not present, these measures may be irrelevant." [1]

In Section II, we will walk you through our set of six strategies for progressive media success in the networked environment. This model incorporates measurement techniques from corporate, public, and online media, as well as prioritizing outcomes over income.

COMPETING VALUE SYSTEMS: METRICS VERSUS MISSION

Independent, progressive media makers often find themselves trapped between two poles. On one hand, they struggle with the need to counter, compete with, and even best commercial outlets. On the other hand, many independent progressive media projects have mission-driven goals: they exist not only to inform but also to empower, elevate, and mobilize their readers, viewers, and listeners. And, always, they struggle to survive.

A brief comparison of measurements for success from two very different media fields—commercial media and community media—demonstrates the traditional dichotomy between profit-driven and mission-driven outlets.

From TiVo, to iTunes, to the switch from analog to digital signals, broadcasters are facing a wholesale transformation of their distribution models. When it became clear that traditional diary and metering methods were no longer adequate to record the consumption habits of audience members, Nielsen Media Research—the global leader in audience measurement—was forced to act. Nielsen met with clients to discuss which metrics they needed, and developed new research methods. As the company's Web site explains:

> We recognize that a well-measured medium is a more valuable medium. And we understand that our measurements of emerging technologies will help the industry develop new business models. . . . At Nielsen Media Research we understand that many of the old ways of doing business just don't work anymore, and we are committed to actively pursuing the development of new measurement services. We also recognize that there can be no "one size fits all" approach to audience measurement.[2]

They call their new model "Anytime Anywhere Media Measurement" (otherwise known as A2/M2). What does this approach involve? Not just measuring in-home television viewing, but measurement and tagging of online streaming video, tracking of digital video recorder and video-on-demand viewing, and branching out into more sophisticated online tracking via the NetRatings arm of the company.

Contrast this intense focus on media consumption to the impact measurements developed by Felicia Sullivan and Dorothy Kidd in "Impact on Our Own Terms," a document published by the Center for International Media Action, a resource center and think tank for social justice media makers. "Impact on Our Own Terms" offers a model for qualitative, mission-driven impact goals, dividing them into several different categories:

- *Individual impacts.* Examples include the number of people who have been trained to create their own media, freedom of expression and creative expression, and increased skill in practices of deliberative and participatory democracy.
- *Organizational impacts.* Examples include the increase in the number of people who access the organization's resources, new partnerships and collaborations, and increased media content of narratives of underserved and marginalized communities.
- *Community impacts.* Examples include the increase in volunteer efforts, new means of sharing knowledge for a common purpose, and the lessons about alternative remedies (i.e., practical case studies) that make practice more effective.

Much like these community media makers, progressive outlets have traditionally taken pride in the fact that they rely on neither corporate backing nor government funding, and that advertising dollars, while important, do not influence editorial coverage or decision making.

While there are some large for-profit independent media projects, many are either noncommercial or verging on becoming volunteer-run. But no matter their size or budget, they all have to be able to explain their impact in order to get people to invest in the organization.

A NEW MEDIA ORDER

By late 2008, the paradigm for assessing what constituted a successful media brand, story, or message was in serious flux.

At the start of the twenty-first century, the U.S. media system seemed to operate according to a predictable power structure. Mass media dominated the national news space: large urban newspapers such as the *New York Times* and the *Washington Post*, national news magazines such as *Time* and *U. S. News & World Report*, TV networks, twenty-four-hour cable news outlets, and radio news and talk shows. Both broadcast and print were expensive and physically limited distribution models. Public broadcasting, community radio, ethnic media, independent magazine and book publishing, alternative newsweeklies, independent film, and other underfunded efforts all worked to fill in the gaps in mainstream media coverage and ideology, and to reach underserved audiences. While the growing popularity of the Internet had opened up many new opportunities for publishers to reach broader audiences more cheaply, and for organizers to begin to experiment with decentralized outreach, only a few online-only publications, including *Slate* and *Salon*, had achieved the same level of legitimacy as the legacy outlets.

This meant that in order to make an impact—to help set the news agenda, influence policy, and introduce issues into the national debate—journalists, newsmakers, and politicians had to aim for coverage or airtime in mainstream outlets. Editors, producers, bookers, and reporters all served as gatekeepers, choosing which topics and figures to cover and which to dismiss. In this system, audiences were often constructed as passive receivers of information, and outlets provided expertise, coverage, and parameters for legitimate debate, determining what "all the news that's fit to print" included. Other ideas were ghettoized into "alternative" or "radical" outlets and given fewer resources and less respect.

Today, the picture is much more complicated. While mainstream outlets still set the national news agenda, it doesn't stay set for long. The pace of the news cycle has accelerated to nearly real time, with multiple, intersecting inputs now feeding and shaping the national discourse. Online, the dynamics of legitimacy keep shifting, with Web-only sources on the right and the left gaining on the traditional agenda-setting news outlets in terms of both traffic and perceived influence. As New York University's Jay

Rosen noted in his PressThink blog in early 2009, "The authority of the press to assume consensus, define deviance, and set the terms for legitimate debate is weaker when people can connect horizontally around and about the news."[3]

This map of the U. S. political blogosphere in June 2008[4] (see p. 54), created by social media analytics firm Linkfluence, suggests the new shape of what Harvard Internet scholar Yochai Benkler calls the "networked public sphere." The playing field, while not yet level, has evened out as content, audiences, and creators from newspapers, TV, film, and new platforms such as blogs all converge online.

"The mass-mediated public sphere used to concentrate the production of stories about who we are, what challenges face us, and how we might overcome them," writes Benkler in *Rebooting America: Ideas for Redesigning American Democracy for the Internet Age*, an anthology of essays published by the Personal Democracy Forum blog. He continues:

> The public at large was reduced to passivity in this model of production; we were no more than "eyeballs." The networked public sphere is comprised of e-mails and e-mail lists, blogs ranging from individual thoughts to professional and semi-professional new voices like Instapundit or Talking Points Memo, to vast collaboration platforms like DailyKos with thousands of contributors, or flash campaigns that repurpose other platforms. . . . A dozen or more years of experience with the networked public sphere has taught us a lot about how it can operate. It is not, it turns out, the republic of yeoman authors that some hoped it would be. But neither is it the trackless cacophony of antagonistic echo chambers that others predicted. Instead, we have seen a public sphere where millions, rather than hundreds or thousands, can participate in setting the agenda, filtering what is important, and telling our common stories. Not everyone; but a large

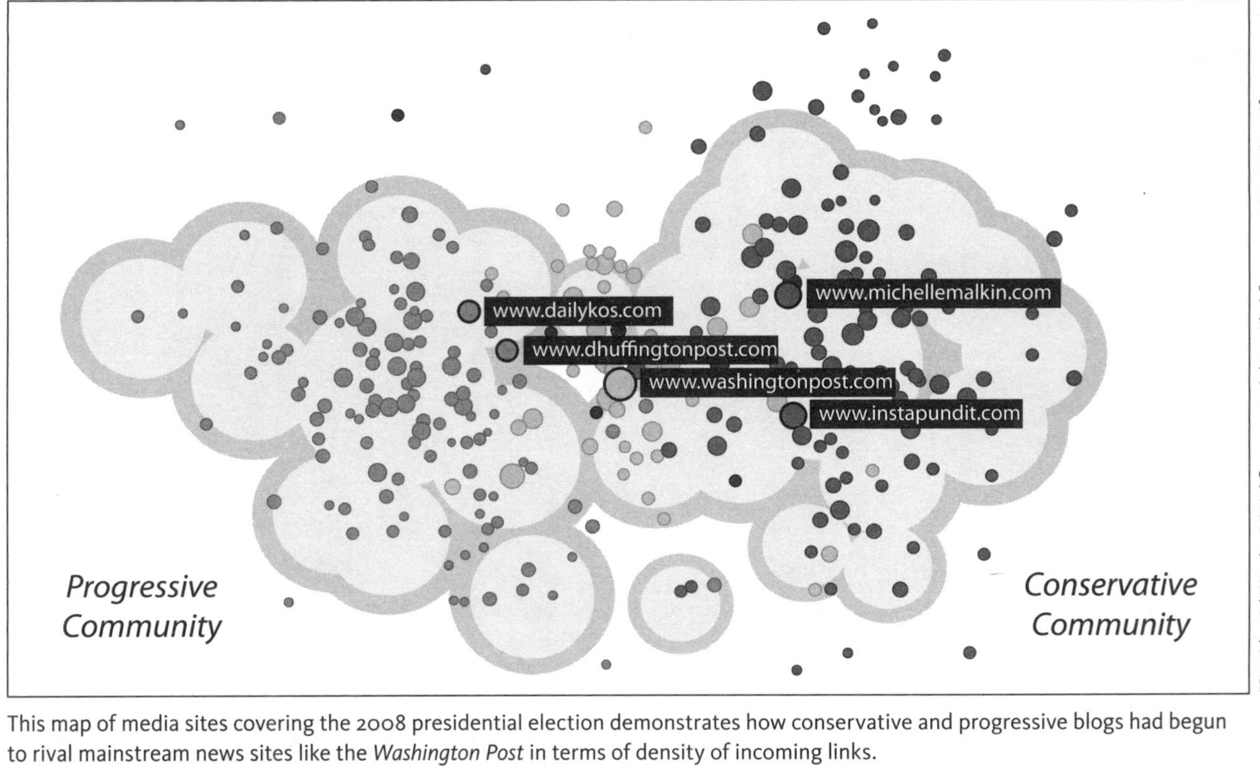

This map of media sites covering the 2008 presidential election demonstrates how conservative and progressive blogs had begun to rival mainstream news sites like the *Washington Post* in terms of density of incoming links.

"Presidential Watch 08," Linkfluence, 2008, http://linkfluence.net/images/pw.gif

and significant change from where we were a mere decade ago."[5]

Despite all of this upheaval, traditional and outdated impact measurements are still often used to evaluate progressive media influence, effectiveness, and credibility. We suggest that independent progressive media projects must track not just commercial metrics—audience numbers, advertising dollars, references from other media outlets, viewership numbers, Web site visits and click-throughs—but also factors that demonstrate they've met their mission. These include:

- *Buzz.* It's not enough for media outlets to just produce content; it is critical for that reporting to move beyond its core audience into the larger public debate. Media outlets can now pursue viral distribution opportunities, including reprints and links on other Web sites, as well as more traditional coverage and discussion of their reporting or analysis on radio, on television, and online. Buzz helps bring new audiences to these outlets and sets the stage for the next phase of success.
- *Credibility.* So the story has gotten out into the world. Now what? For a story, outlet, or campaign to gain traction, the users must trust the source. Audiences can range from everyday citizens to targeted communities, other media outlets, social justice and/or political organizations, and last but not least, policy makers. Trust in the validity of the reporting, the acuity of the analysis, or the integrity of the reporter itself is key to overall impact.
- *Influence.* Influence has always been a key benchmark for journalists, as measured by professional awards and conventions. Winning a Pulitzer, scooping a competitor, or securing a book contract are all markers of influence, well understood in commercial and independent reporting

alike. But progressive media makers have specific reasons to strive for influence: to create a sustainable progressive majority; to inform or shift policy; to unseat conservative foes; to fight for social, gender, and racial justice; and more. Strategies for gaining and amplifying influence in the networked public sphere are evolving rapidly, involving more collaborations, audience engagement, and new tactics for attracting and leveraging attention. Developing strategies that reflect these new practices is paramount for media makers seeking to drive investment.

- *Engagement.* Tactics for encouraging direct audience involvement in shaping or discussing a media project have become much more sophisticated over the years, and easier to roll out. Online tools have lowered the barriers, inviting millions of new participants into the process. But now engagement is no longer an afterthought; it's built into the entire production process, from project design to fund-raising to distribution. Engaged users are creating and curating content, collaborating with media makers on investigation and dissemination, and conducting critiques and discussions about both mainstream and progressive media across a range of sites and platforms. Encouraging and assessing engagement will be increasingly important as the boundaries between makers and users continue to blur.

Just as investors buy stocks in companies to make a profit, users and supporters of progressive media are looking for a return on their investment in the form of social and political impact. The users' investments—of money, time, trust, and action—drive the overall relevance and impact of the media outlet.

Both users and funders are prompted to invest in progressive outlets because they believe in the media outlet's mission. Buzz, credibility, influence, and engagement are all components of high-impact political progressive media. But how do progressive media create the impact? What are the steps and strategies to success? To answer those questions, we've crafted a set of mission-based strategies specifically targeted to progressive media projects.

STRATEGIES FOR HIGH-IMPACT MEDIA

In Section II we provide a new framework for progressive media makers to produce high-impact content and campaigns in the networked media environment. They include:

- *Build progressive network power.* Media outlets, established advocacy organizations, and a rising number of active individuals are forming the new, networked media system. Together, these influential networks can propel a story, issue, or message to reach targeted audiences and/or the mainstream media. In Chapter 4, we examine the rise of the progressive blogosphere and a corresponding network of progressive media outlets, and explore how this sector is organizing itself into both face-to-face and online networks that serve as an infrastructure for increased influence and support.
- *Fight the right.* Many progressive media makers work to refute narratives and assumptions that underlie conservative and mainstream framing of an issue or news story. Approaches range from traditional journalism and analysis to the creation of media projects that, among other things, actively counter, lampoon, or investigate conservative personalities and politicians; mock conservative frames and concerns; and stir up trouble. In Chapter 5, we examine how Brave New Films successfully fights the right through a combination of media production and activation of on-the-ground networks and online organizing, and how they have worked with other emerging projects to counter the Republican Noise Machine.

• *Embrace twenty-first-century muckraking.* Reporters are maintaining and extending a long progressive tradition of investigative journalism in an era when mainstream reporting resources are dwindling. Often this involves new online features and tools—maps, timelines, discussion boards, and interactive databases—all being produced within an increasingly rapid, 24/7 news cycle. In Chapter 6, we examine the transformation of investigative practices through the lens of one innovative project, Talking Points Memo, and the shifting economics of investigation within the mainstream media sphere.

• *Take it to the Hill.* Some media projects or campaigns are designed to directly influence policy decisions by elected or appointed decision makers. In Chapter 7 we examine how networked communication tools supported and extended campaigns around key issues in the 2004–8 period, including challenges to the Foreign Intelligence Surveillance Act and efforts to reveal and combat military contracting.

• *Assemble the progressive choir.* A number of progressive media outlets serve to build and mobilize progressive audiences, providing platforms for ongoing debate, reporting, frame setting, and action. In Chapter 8 we examine how legacy progressive outlets are adapting to and harnessing the new media environment, and how powerful new projects such as Firedoglake have arisen to inform and activate users.

• *Move beyond pale, stale, and male.* A number of progressive projects aim to expand and engage networks of users beyond the traditional audience of the progressive media: middle-class, college-educated, older white men. We explore the dynamics of race within progressive media by examining coverage and activism related to the Jena Six trial, and the dynamics of gender by profiling Feministing, a pioneering progressive, feminist blog.

The stories of impact that follow are large and small, but together they represent a significant change for the progressive media's role in the larger ecosystem. We hope the readers of this book and our blog, www.beyondtheecho.net, will take these strategies even further.

SECTION II:
SIX STRATEGIES FOR
HIGH-IMPACT PROGRESSIVE MEDIA

4
BUILD NETWORK-POWERED MEDIA

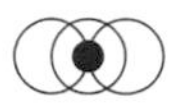

Piercing bells from slot machines. Cocktail waitresses in short, sequined, tight-bodiced dresses. Wads of money being handed over for poker chips and mixed drinks.

Ah, Vegas. Land of sin and parties.

But on a fateful few days in June 2006, if you walked around the corner from the Riviera Hotel and Casino's cavernous gaming space and down a long winding hallway, an entirely different party was happening—a coming-out party, to be exact. Thousands had flocked to Las Vegas for the first Yearly Kos conference. They had gathered out of earnestness, curiosity, and passion for the rising progressive blogosphere.

Political ambitions for the event were high. "These are good, heady days for the people-powered movement," said Markos Moulitsas (aka Kos), founder of one of the most popular liberal blogs, Daily Kos, in his conference address. "We're only four years old. From the early days when bloggers like Atrios and Jerome Armstrong of MyDD inspired me and many other bloggers to stop railing at the television, stop throwing pillows at Hannity and Colmes . . . stop complaining about the pathetic, so-called liberals that were supposedly speaking for us in DC, and take what we felt, that passion, that energy, and start doing it online. We've come a long way since then."[1]

The conference attracted a strange mix of attendees. First there were the so-called A-list bloggers, who had emerged as unlikely celebrities and political experts. They were joined by progressive politicians such as Barbara Boxer and Howard Dean, plus hundreds of other less well-known (but no less impassioned) bloggers and blog community members furious at the Bush administration. While they had argued, agreed on, shared, and dissected political events on a daily basis, for many, this was the first time they had met in person. All were looking to construct a strong progressive movement. They were almost matched in attendance by the pundits, mainstream reporters, and long-in-the-tooth politicos who had came to alternatively cozy up to and mock this group of political and media upstarts.

Why was this event so significant? It was one of the first dynamic public statements by a previously invisible spectrum of the left—young and old, women and men—declaring, "We're here to stay. We're powerful. And we're doing things you can't possibly do." Yearly Kos was the place where the progressive blogosphere announced that they weren't just a set of individuals dallying on the Web anymore, but a growing, strategic, and constructed network dedicated to changing American politics and setting the traditional media world back on its heels.

What happened in Vegas didn't stay in Vegas for long. The mainstream media vied to make sense of this new force, mocking claims by Moulitsas that bloggers would relegate the media and political elite to the "dustbins of history."

"They may think of themselves as rebels, separate from mainstream politics and media," wrote Adam Nagourney of the *New York Times*. "But by the end of a day on which the convention halls were shoulder to shoulder with bloggers, Democratic operatives, candidates and Washington reporters, it seemed that bloggers were well on the way to becoming—dare we say it?—part of the American political establishment. Indeed, the convention, the first of what organizers said would become an annual event, seems on the way to becoming as much a part of the Democratic political circuit as the Iowa State Fair."[2]

STRATEGIC OPPORTUNITIES

The rise of the progressive blogosphere helped to set the stage for today's network-powered media system. It started with impassioned, politically active, and early-adopting individuals, but soon progressive bloggers began to connect with each other online, creating a web of information, mutual links, and organizing muscle. The ongoing impact of the progressive blogosphere is due in large part to bloggers' routine, strategic outreach to the four layers of networks we outlined in Section I, including:

- Networked users
- Self-organized networks
- Institutional networks
- Networks of institutions

But the bloggers are not alone. From 2004 to 2008, legacy progressive outlets, along with grassroots activists, political campaigns, and advocacy organizations, have also worked to reorient themselves to the networked communications environment. Oftentimes this process has reflected familiar offline routines. As a community organizer, President Obama knew that one of the main tenets of building a successful and powerful movement is to start knocking door-to-door in a neighborhood. Organizers ask questions to understand the overlapping issues that the community faces and listen to community members to identify the necessary solutions. Then, one by one, these communities are connected into a larger national campaign.

Throughout the last four years, the same principle has been applied to media organizations. Since 2004, there have been many experiments designed to suss out if and how different components of the progressive media sector might build an infrastructure that would suit the left. Ultimately, few media makers were interested in creating a model that resembled the top-down, lockstep machine that the right had built over the last few decades. Why? Because, as progressives, we believe in debate and diversity and we treasure democratic process.

Instead, the four network layers have evolved to serve as a foundation for the progressive media infrastructure that can rival the right wing's juggernaut. Rather than submitting to a top-down process of defining and disseminating talking points, progressives have built both self-organized and institutionally organized networks that connect clusters of outlets and allies together to identify common issues and move forward with campaigns or projects that can solve those problems. These networks are generally opt-in and can last one day or an entire year. This network-powered media system has emerged as an organic and fluid back-end structure for creating buzz, generating influential campaigns, and engaging users.

Such partnerships can happen organically in the midst of a breaking news story. For example, on September 10, 2008, the Michigan Messenger, a state news site published by the Center for Independent Media, broke the story "Lose Your House, Lose Your Vote," quoting James Carabelli, chairman of the Republican Party in Macomb County, Michigan, as saying, "We will have a list of foreclosed homes and will make sure people aren't voting from those addresses."[3] The implication was that a disproportionate amount of African American families in the area—likely to vote Democratic, and more likely to be in foreclosure as a result of subprime loans—would be disenfranchised. The story quickly spread throughout the blogosphere and into the mainstream media.

A coalition of progressive groups gathered at GOP presidential contender Senator John McCain's headquarters and Macomb County GOP headquarters to protest the "foreclosed voter" plan. ProgressMichigan, a statewide organizing hub for local progressive organizations, and Color of Change, a national online organizing group for black Americans founded by a former MoveOn staffer, both launched a petition drive to stop the practice. The weekend of September 13, Senator Biden campaigned throughout the state on the theme of "lose your house, lose your vote." On September 16, citing the Michigan Messenger story, Senator Obama and the Democratic National Committee filed a lawsuit against the Michigan GOP to stop this practice. The end result? Victory. Both the Democratic and Republican party signed a joint agreement stating neither would use foreclosure lists as a basis for poll challenges in Michigan on election day. The Obama/Biden team won Michigan in the general election.

This was an informal pairing of a media outlet with advocacy networks around a breaking political issue. What happens when there's actual organizing and more formal pipelines of communication?

One successful 2006 campaign suggests how the different layers can work in tandem when deliberately organized together. The Save the Internet coalition organized networked users, self-organized networks, institutional networks, and networks of institutions around the goal of maintaining "network neutrality"—the belief in a free and open Internet and that service providers such as Comcast, AT&T, Verizon, and more should not charge different rates to providers serving up content online. Net neutrality proponents argue that if a tiered system is put in place, consumers will have slow or no access to certain online information (including independent voices).

The Free Press, a nonprofit organization that spearheaded the coalition, regularly featured stories and reports on media reform issues by progressive outlets. Campaigns such as this one provide multiple opportunities for coverage, dissemination, and amplification in the networked communications space.

Tim Karr of Free Press points out that expansive, dynamic grassroots campaigns that draw in many different participants work best when there's a "crisi-tunity"—a looming threat that can be countered by immediate action. Not all policy or social issues have those characteristics, but campaigns like this demonstrate

The network in action

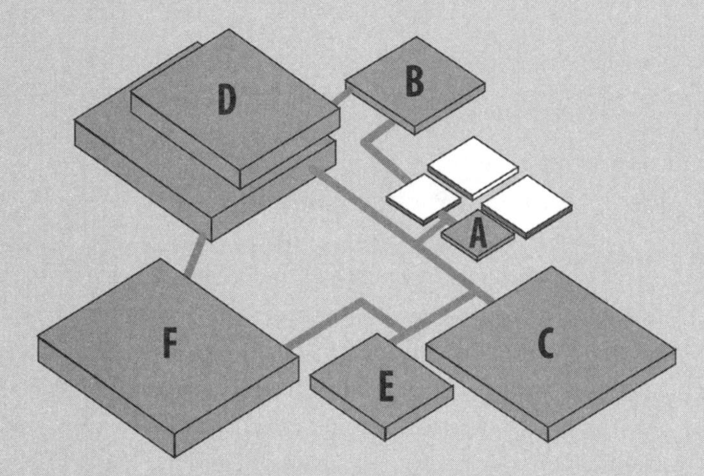

How an issue moves through the network

EXAMPLE: INTERNET FREEDOM—the fight to protect "network neutrality," or a free and open Internet.

A) Media reform organizations like Free Press and the Center for Digital Democracy along with **B)** newsmakers like Common Cause and Consumers Union sounded the first alarms about corporate threats to Internet freedom. **C)** Independent media like *The Nation* and AlterNet.org provided ongoing coverage. Free Press, MoveOn.org and top independent progressive bloggers then formed the SavetheInternet.com coalition. Comprised of more than 700 organizations, the coalition pushed **D)** 750,000 calls, letters and petition signatures to Congress. Within a month **E)** public media like National Public Radio and **F)** mainstream outlets like the *New York Times* reported on the issue. The network did its job: Soon after, there was bipartisan congressional legislation that threatened to derail industry plans.

Jessica Clark and Tracy Van Slyke, "The Emerging Progressive Media Network 2006," *In These Times*, July 2006, http://www.inthesetimes.com/multimedia/mediamap/

Routines for assembling ad hoc campaigns around particular issues evolved during the period we're examining; take for example the coalition that formed around the Savetheinternet.com campaign, described in an outtake from our 2006 map.

the possibilities for creating ad hoc networks that cross all of the different network layers.

MoveOn, a major partner in the coalition, compiled this list of the top ten examples of the grassroots mobilization around net neutrality:

1. Over 850 organizations formed the SavetheInternet.com Coalition—including small businesses, Craig Newmark from Craigslist, consumer groups, non-profits, musicians, and political groups on the left and right.

2. Over 1.6 million people signed a petition to Congress and thousands called Congress, a contrast to the $1 million companies like AT&T and Verizon gave to Senate Commerce Committee members.

3. Grassroots groups from the left and right (like MoveOn and Christian Coalition) mobilized their members to call Congress in support of Net Neutrality.

4. Independent bloggers, YouTube users, and podcasters released cool audio and video.

5. Jon Stewart humorously took on Senator Ted Stevens and told his viewers that eliminating Net Neutrality would create a "two-tiered hierarchy."

6. Non-political groups like college football teams, video gamers, pro-wrestling fans, and ninjas have rallied people for Net Neutrality.

7. Over 20,000 Myspace users and 13,000 Facebook members have joined the fight to preserve Net Neutrality.

8. Artists and musicians like Moby, REM, and OK GO came out for Net Neutrality, and some female singers

called "The Broadband" and wrote a Net Neutrality theme song.

9. 25 Net Neutrality petition deliveries to Senators across the nation in August 2006 made a huge media splash and got 6 new Senators off the fence. Then, in 2007, SavetheInternet.com Coalition members have held over 40 in-district meetings with their local members of Congress and their staff.

10. In 2008, Internet users made Net Neutrality a presidential campaign issue. A user-generated website called 10Questions.com announced that whatever YouTube question had the most votes by the time of an MTV forum with Barack Obama would be asked on national TV. Thousands of Internet users swooped into action, voted for a great question about Net Neutrality, and got the question asked (and answered). This also generated good headlines.[4]

This campaign had all the components of a network-powered media system. In addition, progressive outlets such as *The Nation* and AlterNet covered the story early and often, adding to the buzz that allowed this issue to reach larger audiences. Citizen media makers and independent musicians were also integral to this campaign. It also included many of the strategies we describe in the following chapters.

Infrastructure might just be the least glamorous part of the media system, as it doesn't result in headlines, awards, or fans. But it's important: a dynamic progressive media infrastructure serves as the backbone for making impact. It creates the circuits of communication and coordination—built on trust, debate, information sharing, and action—that can increase the influence and success of the entire sector. Online and offline, networks provide both social and political capital. Infrastructure building can also generate user loyalty across outlets. While individual organizations may talk to their users in terms of their own needs and goals, collectives of institutions and individuals can talk more broadly about shared goals and raise money for multiple organizations and issue coverage across platforms.

By early 2009, not only were progressives getting the hang of building network-powered media, but new participants were streaming into related outlets and platforms. The result was a potent mix of actors driving reporting, analysis, and campaigns into the broader public debate. Some choose to overtly coordinate around messages, reporting, and campaigns, while others form looser networks designed to support conversation, information sharing, and long-term sustainability. The network-powered progressive media infrastructure interweaves both formal, funded collaborations and innovative responses by individuals.

CONSTRUCTING A POWERFUL PROGRESSIVE BLOGOSPHERE

Between 2004 and 2008, the progressive blogosphere's power and influence grew due in large part to the partnerships and alliances its members actively built. They coordinated with other individuals within the blogosphere and organizational allies outside it—not to mention the candidates that they worked (not always successfully) to propel into state and federal legislatures. While not all of those campaigns won, they served as teachable moments, helping to inform the network-powered politics that played a pivotal role in Obama's victory.

A quick review of the progressive blogosphere's interlinked model demonstrates how a network infrastructure can propel both individual and collective impact. By cross-linking, bloggers improved one another's visibility on search engines. By participating in joint advertising networks (such as BlogAds, which launched in 2002) or starting their own (such as CommonSense Media, powered by bloggers from Firedoglake), they have driven revenue to some bloggers, allowing a select few to devote their careers full-time to the blogosphere. By directing their hundreds of thousands of users to make donations to candidates through online donation clearinghouses such as ActBlue, they demonstrated their ability to make or break a candidate. By sharing, contextualizing, and constantly analyzing the news and political and social memes, they built buzz and fought back against the right's noise machine. By strategizing together—both out in the open and behind the scenes on conference calls and listservs—the progressive blogosphere mounted concerted campaigns on issues ranging from Social Security to immigration, wiretapping, and beyond. And by socializing together—at conferences, events, and national meet-up groups such as Drinking Liberally and Laughing Liberally—they wove their political activities into the rest of their lives.

Progressive bloggers also made another decision—based on strategy, temperament, or both—that increased their influence. They focused on attacking high-profile political and media institutions rather than formulating a radical agenda or fomenting on-the-ground protests. This approach was different from the one employed by Indymedia, a worldwide collective of journalists and activists. Contributors used Web-based tools to self-organize decentralized antiglobalization demonstrations, beginning with the groundbreaking response to the 2000 WTO meetings in Seattle. The Indymedia movement also fed the creation of local independent media centers (IMCs) dedicated to grassroots reporting.

In many ways, the Indymedia movement has been shortchanged when it comes to accounts of citizen journalism. Embedded in this dismissal were familiar prejudices against not only radical politics but also counterculture stereotypes lingering from the 1960s. But dismissing the well-known progressive political bloggers was harder—not only were many of them white, male, and professional, but they were essentially playing in the same arena as the pundits and politicians, focusing not on smashing the gates but on crashing them, on widening participation in electoral politics and media coverage.

While many progressives were moved to blog about the Bush administration by 9/11 or the Iraq war, it took a few years for their political influence to build. Articles such as the 2004 *New York Times Magazine* cover story, "Fear and Laptops on the Campaign Trail" show the mixed curiosity and contempt with which the new interlopers were greeted.[5] Throughout the 2006 and 2008 elections, campaign strategists seasoned by the lessons of Howard Dean's presidential campaign both worked and clashed with progressive bloggers in overlapping networks of fund-raising, promotion, and commentary.

While political campaigns drew progressive bloggers together, there was also much internal debate. The individuals in the progressive blogosphere represent the wide political spectrum of the left itself: centrists, populists, anarchists, progressives, fiscal conservatives but social liberals, feminists, people of color, and people of various income levels. Many represent combinations of these political identities, making it harder to silo them into single categories. But throughout Bush's two terms, their shared disgust for the administration bound many of them together and inspired them to pioneer new networked media practices.

This was not traditional journalism, or even the polemic movement literature that nourished and spawned the political organizing of previous generations around civil rights, women's issues, and antiwar movements. Bloggers conflated a variety of practices that used to exist in separate spheres: reporting and analysis, mobilization, "oppo" research, wonky hairsplitting, fact-checking, meme setting, mud-slinging, campaigning, fund-raising, and lobbying. Applying this formula, sites such as Daily Kos, Huffington Post, Open Left, and Firedoglake have grown in relevance and extended well beyond single-author blog formats to include reader diaries and online communities for their users to write, share, rate, and recommend content with and for each other.

Matt Stoller summed up this multiplicity of roles in a MyDD post responding to a mid-2007 article by Jonathan Chait of the *New Republic*. "We don't necessarily distinguish between politics and policy, or activism and journalism, and we don't pretend that there is an above the fray and an 'in the muck,'" wrote Stoller. "Most of all, we respect ideas because ideas, when implemented, have immense power. Ideas matter. Conservative ideas have affected us personally, whether it was growing up in a suburb or having no health care insurance. And to the extent that you create ideas or appropriate ideas and organize around them, you can build a new society. That's what the right did, which is why we respect the right."[6]

By 2008, the blogosphere had reached a pivotal point, rivaling the right wing's long-term media dominance. As MSNBC's blog First Read noted in April 2008, "The left-wing blogosphere is MUCH more powerful than what you see on the right this cycle and it reminds us of the advantage Bush had in '04. While we all know about that so-called right-wing voice machine, don't forget that there is now a left-wing noise machine (on the internet) as well. And it has found its voice."[7]

Jon Henke of the conservative QandO Blog expanded on this statement, writing enviously:

> The Left has a well-organized blogosphere that can do three things for Progressive candidates:
>
> 1. Messaging—between Moveon.org, the blogs and the many issue-advocacy outfits, the Leftosphere has a very powerful communication mechanism for candidates and issues. They have messaging and distribution capacity and it is well-coordinated with advocacy and awareness elements of their coalition.
>
> 2. Money—the Presidential money is high-profile and not every candidate gets a lot of online money, but the Left-

> roots can move significant sums of money to the challengers that hit the right notes, make the right friends, and jump into the hot progressive issues. They have succeeded in tapping the long tail to move fundraising—and the financial incentive machine—outside of the establishment channels.
>
> 3. Mobilization—the Progressives are passionate, energized, over their ideas. They have a story they're excited about, they have effectively tied their stories together and they're tightly wedded to the (dangerous) tactic of populism. They're unified around that mission, so they can and do mobilize people. Again, that moves significant power outside the traditional channels.
>
> The Leftroots can deliver messaging, money and mobilization, so Democratic candidates become path-dependent on them. They have sufficient power to move politicians to their ideas.[8]

Say it again, brother.

LEGACY PROGRESSIVE MEDIA LOOK INWARD TO CREATE IMPACT

As the blogosphere grew in impact and began to gain grudging recognition from both the corporate media and the political establishment, many in legacy progressive media organizations recognized that it was time to start looking internally to reimagine their own paths. They noted that the success and influence of the blogosphere was driven in part by the fact that the bloggers were not bound by traditional journalism practices. Bloggers could both align themselves with one another and other organizations on issue campaigns and advocate and fund-raise for politicians.

There was also a different generational response to attitudes toward communication and advocacy provided by new online platforms. In a commentary on *New York Times* magazine writer Matt Bai's book *The Argument: Billionaires, Bloggers, and the Battle to Remake Democratic Politics*, Micah Sifry of the Personal Democracy Forum wrote in September 2007:[9]

> As Bai points out, many of the younger bloggers who are the leaders of the netroots (as opposed to the footsoldiers who read and comment on the blogs, but don't have the ability to quit their jobs and start new lives as netroots activists) tend to be in the twenties and early thirties, and thus stand a generation apart from the mostly middle-aged lefties and liberals who run big advocacy organizations and edit the opinion journals. The older, more established types have spent most of their adult lives aiming their arguments at elite audiences and thus have generally been slow to recognize and embrace the new energy flowing through the netroots.

Critics from both mainstream and legacy outlets accused the bloggers of threatening journalistic integrity and reducing politics to polemics, while proponents argued that a more genteel approach weakened progressives' effectiveness in a cutthroat national discourse. Feminist and ethnic media commentators often argued that the rise of new "A-list" bloggers re-created the white, male punditocracy, contradicting progressive rhetoric about diversity and restricting political focus to electoral politics.

The tensions between the multiple sectors of the progressive media have dissipated quite a bit over the last few years as legacy outlets, recognizing that journalism models were changing with or without them, integrated blogging into their sites. Meanwhile, it had become increasingly clear that the national blogosphere could not produce in-depth journalism and conduct investigations as consistently and thoroughly as established progressive media institutions. They needed each other.

The next barrier to building media infrastructure came down to money. The funding and revenue pool for progressive media institutions was small. The scramble for resources had left many individual outlets in constant competition. Large liberal foundations had little understanding of the role that media played in politics, and often would not fund content or outlets. As a result, they saw each other as rivals for audiences, resources, and influence within the larger public and political debate. But with the rise of the Internet, few outlets could hope to be the kings of the castle. Every individual, not just institutions, now had the ability to command their own castle.

So what was the infrastructure model that would work for the legacy progressive media? And what would help support their adaptation to the changing media landscape? In late 2005 and throughout 2006, the editors and publishers from *Mother Jones*, the *American Prospect*, and *The Nation*, leaders from Link TV, Free Speech TV, and AlterNet, and others gathered in response to the question of how and why progressive media didn't make the desired impact on the 2004 election.

As more and more diverse individuals and media outlets were brought to the table throughout the next few years at in-person meetings, a consensus emerged. It was time to create a network of progressive media outlets that would be able to both amplify independent journalism's voice in broader public debates about the crucial political and social issues of our time and navigate the wave of profound technological change reshaping both the media business and the practice of journalism itself.

In 2006, The Media Consortium was officially born. This network of progressive outlets, based at the Foundation for National Progress (the nonprofit parent of *Mother Jones* magazine), vowed to "amplify our voices; increase our collective clout; leverage our current audience and reach out to new ones; transform our sector's position in a rapidly changing media and political environment; and redefine ourselves and progressivism for a new century."

One of the first joint experiments was to determine the size and depth of the progressive media audience. Sixteen consortium members agreed to pour their various lists—subscribers, donors, registered online users, newsletter subscribers, and so on—into a single file. A third party cleaned up the file, ran a series of demographic overlays on the data, and reported that:

- These sixteen organizations had a combined file size of 2.9 million names (about the same size as MoveOn's file): 1.8 million confirmed regular-mail names and 1.1 million confirmed e-mail addresses.
- Only one in four names on the original list is shared between two or more organizations. In other words, 75 percent of the original list is served by only one media outlet, meaning there is very little audience crossover.

The size of the file alone demonstrated that, collectively, the sector has an audience of significant influence. It also suggested that the progressive media had real opportunities to grow its audience, which could have a critical effect on the economic models of these organizations and the impact and reach of their journalism.

Since that time, The Media Consortium has helped to launch multiple coordinated editorial and business projects for journalism-focused media outlets to help build the impact of their independent reporting and analysis, continue to expand their audiences, and explore ways to integrate new technologies into their work. These projects are identified and designed by network members, rather than being dictated by ideologically motivated funders or cooked up in think tanks like the right's talking points.

In 2008, the progressive blogosphere's political power combined with the strength of newly organized legacy progressive outlets to significantly influence political and public dialogue and support outstanding journalism. But there was one additional ingredient added to the mix that would move this rising network to the next level. What was it? We hate to be corny, but it's true: it was you.

HEY, YOU

From 2006 to 2008, the influx of new, free, and ever-simpler social media and tools—YouTube, Facebook, MyBarackObama.com, Twitter, and on—prompted individuals to flood the Web with their own commentary and form new networks for action.

As Peter Daou, a longtime blogger and Internet director for Senator Hillary Clinton's presidential bid, wrote in a late 2008 retrospective for the Publius Project of Harvard's Berkman Center for Internet and Society:

> If there's one thing that makes the 2008 election an inflection point, it is this: that the context, perception, and course of events is fundamentally changed by the collective behavior of the Internet's innumerable opinion-makers. Every piece of news and information is instantly processed by the combined brain power of millions, events are interpreted in new and unpredictable ways, observations transformed into beliefs, thoughts into reality. Ideas and opinions flow from the ground up, insights and inferences, speculation and extrapolation are put forth, then looped and re-looped on a previously unimaginable scale, conventional wisdom created in hours and minutes. This wasn't the case during the last presidential election—the venues and the voices populating them hadn't reached critical mass. They have now."[10]

On a day-to-day, minute-by-minute level, activated citizens connected with each other through SMS messages, listservs, e-mail, online chats, and a myriad of social networking sites. Online conversations and direct messages were filled with notices about breaking news, tactical and philosophical arguments, debates on the merits and demerits of candidates and incumbents, rapid response to the latest right-wing distortions, and last but not least, ongoing proactive planning to coordinate even more opportunities to report, analyze, share, and highlight issues or events.

Once, much of this sort of political reporting and analysis only happened in top-down, legacy media organizations. The blogosphere "crashed the gates" of traditional media power. But networked social media systems are now decimating any walls left between engaged users and media makers. While independent media have always prided themselves on being the voice for the voiceless, underrepresented populations now have the opportunity to sing at the top of their lungs and be heard by millions.

As you read the following chapters, you will see multiple examples of how the various network layers come into play, driving pivotal moments of political change.

5
FIGHT THE RIGHT

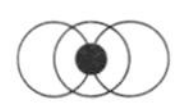

On August 14, 2008, with merely eleven days left before the Democratic National Convention, presidential election coverage had hit a state of perpetual siege.

The latest uproar? The media was abuzz over the new book *Obama Nation*, the latest from Jerome R. Corsi, a conservative writer best known for his co-authorship of the 2004 book *Unfit for Command.* During the previous election cycle, that book launched the damaging "Swift boat" attacks against Senator John Kerry, which cast doubt on the Democratic presidential candidate's military record. Backed by the Fox drumbeat, conservative book clubs, talk radio squawkers, and complicit mainstream commentators, Corsi's 2004 attack on Kerry had worked so well that "swiftboating" became its own verb.

A glance at Google News that day offered a scrolling breakdown of corporate media reactions to the release of *Obama Nation*:

> *5 hours ago*: Bill O'Reilly claims that the book is number one on the best-seller list because Americans know little about Obama. He cites the candidate's refusal to come on to his show as proof that "the senator simply will not sit for challenging interviews."
>
> *4 hours ago*: *The Boston Globe* reports on a Democratic National Committee online campaign to dismiss the book as "rehashed distortions and the same old lies."

3 hours ago: A *Chicago Sun-Times* columnist accuses Corsi of "racial fear-mongering."

30 minutes ago: CBS News reports that the Obama camp will "hit back hard."

Would the right wing's smear machine effectively take down another Democratic presidential candidate?

Not this time. As usual, when it came to fighting back against the right, Brave New Films (BNF) was in the middle of the action. Like clockwork, an e-mail arrived in our in-boxes, titled "How to Stop the Smears Against Obama." Signed by "Robert Greenwald and the Brave New Team," it featured a video debunking Fox News mischaracterizations of Obama, with instructions on how to forward the video to friends, ramp up its popularity on social media sites, get it on local TV, and sign a related petition. "In the coming weeks, FOX will escalate its gross misrepresentations of Obama, and we know from painful past experience that some in the corporate media will spread FOX's canards by presenting them as fact. We must stop the spread," Greenwald wrote.[1]

STRATEGIC OPPORTUNITIES

BNF has become one of the most visible hubs in the loosely linked network of media projects that now serve as progressive shock troops, anticipating and responding to conservative attacks.

Vowing not to repeat the 2004 loss in 2008, major progressive donors sank millions of dollars into organizations designed to mount concentrated campaigns against conservative media. While some of these didn't seem like media outlets at first—notably, the Center for American Progress and Media Matters for America—they have developed influential and relentless blogs that match their conservative counterparts post for post. What's more, private investors and foundations have helped to bankroll a multiplatform array of for-profit progressive media projects. In contrast to the dry, "reality-based" communications style that liberals and lefties had favored in the past, these new progressive media efforts became funnier, more interactive, and more accessible to a broad swath of people.

Outlets that identify fighting the right as a major mission can make an impact in a number of ways. By "poking the bear," targeting right-wing personalities, they create reactions from their targets, generating ripple effects that can bring stories and perspectives to light in the mainstream press. They also successfully challenge conservative smears, talking points, and claims. They anticipate conservative reactions and "inoculate" audiences against them, introducing frames in advance that might otherwise not have gained traction. At its best, fighting the right can advance progressive frames and introduce critical reporting and information while neutralizing the right. What's more, fighting the right has become a joint effort—many progressive media makers have learned to work together to build buzz, promote one another, connect around campaigns and issues, and focus on victory over nuance.

In many ways, founder Robert Greenwald's path mirrors the trajectory of the most visible progressive media projects of the period. Because he initially achieved success in the commercial world, rather than through traditional lefty media, he was not hampered by movement conventions or qualms about ideological purity. His team can also actively and overtly push against certain conservative candidates and prop up progressive candidates under their PAC umbrella—which is a clear distinction from other nonprofit media outlets, which are legally barred from such activities.

Like the progressive bloggers, Greenwald and BNF make no apologies for their political commitments. These proactive media projects broke the "just the facts" mold, meshing opposition research, media criticism, and political organizing—from individual projects such as Crooks and Liars, a pioneering video blog that dissects mainstream news clips from a progressive angle, to national broadcast efforts such as Air America, which pits itself against the big talkers of the right: Limbaugh, Imus, Hannity, Savage, Beck, and their smaller-fry ilk.

BNF has drawn freely from both the worlds of organizing and entertainment, borrowing what works and inventing new routines and channels. Tracy Fleischman, BNF's former communications director, told us that the organization's success is based on its ability to "put a picture on things in a very visual culture."

Greenwald's work joins that of a slate of engaged progressive documentarians, from Michael Moore to Al Gore, who have given the form more ideological bite. Their innovations have influenced the formats of political advertising and cable news shows such as *Countdown*, dovetailing with the efforts of satirical shows including *The Daily Show* and *The Colbert Report* to form a new genre of political communication.

The Corsi book gave the fighting-the-right battalion a chance to shine during the 2008 election cycle. Published on August 1 by Simon & Schuster's Threshold Editions (an imprint edited by Republican operative Mary Matalin), *Obama Nation* was the tip of a long spear aimed squarely at the candidate's reputation. In it, Corsi questioned Obama's citizenship, suggested that he had been a practicing Muslim, and insinuated that he had dealt drugs.[2] As the *New York Times* reported somewhat indignantly, Corsi's screed debuted at the top of the paper's bestseller list, "pushed along by a large volume of bulk sales, intense voter interest in Mr. Obama and a broad marketing campaign that has already included 100 author interviews with talk radio hosts across the country."[3]

For weeks, multiple progressive media, fact-checking, and advocacy organizations battled conservatives' all-out efforts to push Corsi's book into the mainstream narrative. Bloggers and watchdog organizations such as Media Matters for America tirelessly worked to break down every smear Corsi made about Obama.[4] Media Matters' Paul Waldman appeared on multiple radio and television shows, often opposite Corsi, to point out the ludicrous claims posited in the book and Corsi's own history of questionable veracity.

"Let's put this in some historical context," Waldman told Larry King in a mid-August face-off with the author. "Four years ago, Mr. Corsi co-wrote a book called *Unfit for Command* that was part of the Swift Boat Veterans for Truth campaign against John Kerry. Every single objective observer that looked at that came to the conclusion that it was just riddled with falsehoods, distortions and unbelievable claims. Now, four years later, he has come out with *another* book that is just riddled with distortions and falsehoods. So the question is: Why on earth would anyone listen to what he has to say about Barack Obama?"[5]

Even Kerry, who was derided in the previous presidential campaign cycle for reacting too slowly to the attacks, struck back while the iron was hot to defend Obama, launching TruthFightsBack.com. Organizations ranging from *The Nation* to No More Mister Nice Blog denounced the book and its conservative backers. As Jennifer Nix wrote on the Huffington Post:

> Let's do worst first, and review the life-so-far of a book that is truly the avatar of wingnut-inspired foolishness, incredulity, darkness and despair: *Obama Nation* by WorldNet Daily writer and swift-boating smear-lackey Jerome Corsi. This 384-page menace of malicious libel and slander was ushered onto the *New York Times* and Amazon bestseller lists by longtime GOP hack-cum-editor Mary-Mrs.-James-Carville-Matalin, aided by bulk buys from right-wing membership groups and the Conservative Book Club, and via right-wing talk radio and Fox News Channel. It has now received nearly two straight weeks of saturation mainstream media coverage, including a front-page news story and excerpt in the *Times*.[6]

Nix was spoiling for a head-to-head battle in mainstream outlets between *Obama Nation* and *Obama's Challenge*, a book by Robert Kuttner, the co-founder of progressive policy magazine the *American Prospect.*[7] Publisher Chelsea Green (where Nix worked as a marketer and editor from 2004 to 2006) had rushed Kuttner's manuscript into production in order to counter preelection takedowns of the candidate.

But book publishing was just one front in the perpetual political media war. By late 2008, other elements of the progressive media rapid response network had also fallen into place. Cable news, long dominated by conservative and centrist talking heads, began to break open. Keith Olbermann's viewership tripled between 2004 and 2008, growing much more quickly than the audience of his conservative rivals Bill O'Reilly and Lou Dobbs. Rachel Maddow—who got her start on Air America—launched a second popular progressive news show on MSNBC, beating Larry King's numbers in her second week of broadcast.[8]

Progressive radio, too, was on the upswing.[9] "Having grown in both influence and audience, progressive talk radio has begun to push back against the worst excesses of radical right-wing talk," writes Rory O'Connor in *Shock Jocks: Hate Speech and Talk Radio.*

> The left talkers are also finding themselves accompanied for the first time by a nascent and newly potent independent media infrastructure. With the Internet as a sort of progressive counterpart to conservative talk radio, there are now literally hundreds of aggressive left-leaning blogs, many written by top journalists, as well as progressive news-aggregating Web sites such as Huffington Post, AlterNet, Salon, Raw Story, BuzzFlash, Common Dreams and others. . . . This independent media challenge not only confronts dangerous hate speech, but also tackles the echoes and distortions that lead to an information gap for consumers of both corporate and conservative media in the United States.[10]

How did all of this develop? A dissection of BNF's long-running anti-Fox campaign illustrates how strategies for fighting the right evolved in the networked media environment.

2004–6: DOC FILMS ON THE OFFENSIVE

Greenwald's crusade against Fox News and all it represents has transformed with the times, riding shifts in popular sentiment and the cascade of new participatory technologies. Spanning more than four years and a myriad of platforms, Greenwald's campaign began with the 2004 release of *Outfoxed: Rupert Murdoch's War on Journalism*, which he directed and produced. Along the way, Greenwald and his team have pioneered new hybrids of audience-based outreach and distribution; forged a series of potent alliances with progressive activists, bloggers, media makers, nonprofits, and media monitors; and established a range of "Brave New" organizations, including BNF, Brave New Theaters, the Brave New PAC, and the Brave New Foundation, which has a mission to "[champion] social justice issues by using media to inspire, empower, motivate and teach civic participation that makes a difference."

Brave New Film's producers often find themselves in the metaphorical trenches. Not only do they dig up dirt on greedy corporations and conservative politicians, they aptly zing back at mud slung. It all started with Greenwald producing the 2002 film *Unprecedented: The 2000 Presidential Election*, which examined the Florida recount controversy. But in 2004, Greenwald upped the ante and strategically chose high-profile targets in order to leverage the news cycle in that election year by releasing a series of documentaries. These included *Uncovered: The War on Iraq*, which featured interviews with diplomats and intelligence officers skeptical about the Bush administration's rationale for the Iraq invasion; *Unconstitutional: The War on Our Civil Liberties*, which investigated the government's curtailment of civil liberties after Congress passed the Patriot Act in 2001; and *Outfoxed.*

Greenwald is a short, energetic, and gregarious man in his early sixties. He courts controversy with an infectious grin, and makes media that match his personality—hard-hitting and politically engaged, with flashes of humor and few pretensions to subtlety or high aesthetics. Unlike other guerilla documentarians of the last few years—for example, Michael Moore or Morgan Spurlock—Greenwald doesn't place himself in the middle of the story. Instead, he relies on cameos by both experts and everyday people to score hits and evoke empathy.

Before he began his run of documentaries, Greenwald produced commercially successfully TV and film for three decades. While critics such as Bill O'Reilly mock him for work such as *Xanadu*, now a cult favorite, his work has garnered nominations for several Emmy and Golden Globe awards, and the American Film Institute named him the 2002 Producer of the Year.[11]

Coming from the big-budget realm of Hollywood, Greenwald was stymied at first by the hardscrabble doc-film economics. More than once he's self-financed his productions. With each documentary, he learned new lessons about what it takes to fund and distribute openly political films in a hostile marketplace. Lacking the muscle of a big studio's buzz builders, he partnered with organizations such as MoveOn, AlterNet, and the Center for American Progress to put DVDs directly into the hands of concerned progressives. With MoveOn's help, *Outfoxed* premiered at more than three thousand "house parties" around the country before it ever hit theatrical release. At $10 each, the DVDs became both an income source and a form of currency, serving as swag at fundraisers and subscription drives for other progressive media outlets. More interested in political punch than critical acclaim or box office numbers, Greenwald told the *San Francisco Chronicle* that this method was "the best way to get material out there quickly. . . . I think there's a real value in energizing the choir."[12]

Piggybacking on engagement strategies that other independent documentarians had honed over the last three decades,

Greenwald's team began to conceptualize the films primarily as vehicles for outreach, collaboration, and publicity events—the hub of issue-based campaigns rather than an end in themselves. The rise of the political blogosphere and citizen-driven networking and promotion tools provided new avenues for outreach at a speed that matched the 24/7 news cycle.

In a September 2007 interview, Greenwald told *Cineaste*:

> As I know from my long career in the commercial world, gatekeepers—be they good, bad, or indifferent—don't move quickly: whether it's a cable, or network, or theatrical release, getting a film out is a long, slow process. But it was also the case with the first film, *Uncovered*, that we wanted it to be timely. Remember that, back then, people weren't making politically timely documentaries: ours was really one of the first where we said, "We're not going to do a documentary ten years from today, we're doing it now, we want it out now and we want to affect the political dialog now." That whole concept of immediacy was a breakthrough.[13]

Jim Gilliam, a former dot-com executive who helped to produce *Uncovered* and *Outfoxed*, joined Greenwald in his efforts to juice up the distribution cycle. Gilliam, who is in his early thirties, is a pale and gangly six foot nine to Greenwald's sturdy five foot six. He brought invaluable online organizing experience to the mix.[14] Gilliam understands how intrinsic the Web has become to many people's lives; he started his personal blog back in 1999. He has been instrumental to developing both online fund-raising and research strategies for the films, marrying his netroots sensibility to Greenwald's time in Hollywood.

Bush's unwelcome 2004 victory prompted Greenwald and Gilliam to found Brave New Films, solidifying their commitment to producing "strategic documentaries."[15] The production company's first project was the feature-length 2005 film *Wal-Mart: The High*

Cost of Low Price, which attacked the big-box store's dubious labor practices and predatory land grabs. The planning process for the film began with identifying organizational partners that could use it to address the issues of their members. By the end, BNF staffers connected with more than four hundred organizations, including the Service Employees International Union (SEIU), the National Council of Churches, and the Young Progressive Majority.

They also coordinated with progressive outlets and bloggers to generate coverage during the film's November premiere week. This also marked one of The Media Consortium's first attempts at editorial coordination, in which *In These Times*, *The Nation*, the *American Prospect*, and AlterNet all published different articles on the same day tackling different themes and stories raised by the documentary on Wal-Mart's practices. Each of the media outlets linked to the other three media organizations' stories—which now seems like a no-brainer but at the time was a giant leap forward in collaboration and connection for these media organizations.

The premiere-week coverage had a different theme each day: Sunday was "A Moral Approach," in which BNF connected with different churches around the country to screen the film; Monday was "Shareholder Day," in which demands to Wal-Mart were released on Wall Street; and on and on. Throughout the week, the documentary was screened in thousands of churches, small businesses, schools, and private homes. More than 850 volunteer "field producers" pitched in to help research, gather images, and spread the word about the film.

Greenwald and company estimate that in one week there were seven thousand screenings attended by some 500,000 people. According to a 2006 article by Kimberley Brown of *Realscreen*, the planners dubbed it the "biggest grassroots mobilization in movie history." Comparing the film to similar media projects, she noted, "While Moore is a preacher, Greenwald is a shepherd. And his flock keeps getting bigger."[16] By reaching out to viewers and venues not traditionally associated with progressive politics, the film was able to spark real debate. Greenwald told *Cineaste*:

> I think that galvanizing the base is very positive, and that's really what I thought when I started the films. When you charge eight, nine, or ten dollars to see it in a movie theater, you will never get anybody other than the base. It's an impossibility. It's hard enough to get people to pay when they love the subject, or they're behind you. But what we discovered with alternative distribution is that if we make hundreds of thousands of DVDs available to people, we're getting way beyond the base. If it shows in a church, they're not checking your political agenda. If it's at a school, if it's at a union hall, if it's at a bowling parlor, if it's at a pizza parlor, if it's at a family gathering, it moves beyond the regular.[17]

What's more, the film itself was just the tip of the iceberg. A multiplatform project, the campaign included a companion book; a slate of online resources for activists; a set of short videos designed to highlight particular issues, including satirical commercials; and an ongoing blog, tracking victories against Wal-Mart and new strikes against the company.[18]

What was the impact? The film has been cited as a key factor in employee battles for health care, and in grassroots campaigns to pass "big-box ordinances" to keep the company out of communities. Other reactions were less salutary: Rupert Murdoch's *New York Post* compared Greenwald to Nazi propagandist Joseph Goebbels, and Wal-Mart hired a bevy of consultants to fact-check and denounce Greenwald's previous films. But BNF courted the right-wing reaction, which only helped to raise the profile of the documentary.

BNF produced a few more long-form documentaries released in 2006, including *Iraq for Sale: The War Profiteers*, a documentary on the excesses of private contractors such as Halliburton, Blackwater Security Consulting, and CACI International in the Iraq war. The film featured firsthand accounts from soldiers, widows, and contractors about how private contracting wasted taxpayer dollars and placed employees in harm's way. It also sketched ties between the private companies and Bush administration insiders.

The release of the film is what led to Greenwald's testifying in front of Congress (as described in the introduction). Fleischman notes that this was a critical moment: "Progressive media really became the source of reporting on war profiteering."

Greenwald believes one of the major reasons that they have impact is that they are able to jump early into a campaign before it's become mainstream. But BNF frames their productions differently based on their goals, which reside in either activating the base or converting the undecided. For example, Greenwald says, *Outfoxed* was developed, framed, and distributed based on activating the base, while *Iraq for Sale* was designed more for the undecided. Either way, they are geared to get a response. "Robert Greenwald's documentaries are like sledgehammers of rage against everything he finds wrong with America, including Wal-Mart, Fox News and the Bush administration," wrote Jeannette Catsoulis in a *New York Times* review. "He wants to rile us up, and he's not subtle. But then, neither are his targets."[19]

Iraq for Sale became Brave New Film's first people-powered film. Short of dollars, as usual, Gilliam got the idea to raise money from the production company's fans and e-mail lists. He sent out the appeal for funds to produce the documentary before the filming had even begun. An anonymous donor committed $100,000 on the condition that someone else match it with $200,000. "That someone else is you!" Gilliam e-mailed. "4,000 people giving $50 each. We'll put everyone's name in the credits." Within 10 days they had raised $267,892.

"For all practical purposes, this is the first time I've heard of raising money for a film this way. I've got to hand it to them. I'm very impressed. It's clever," Lawrence Turman, a veteran Hollywood producer of over forty films told the *Washington Post* in an article by William Booth. "This is the Howard Dean School of Film Funding," wrote Booth, "very Net-rooty, very social-networky, very now. It promises Hollywood dreams beyond the reach of the Man."[20]

The new business model marked a dramatic turn for the organization, setting a benchmark for future fund-raising efforts. It also put the power of media creation in the hands of the audience, giving them a vested interest in making sure the documentary was successful. Gilliam developed a related Web site called Brave New Theaters.[21] The site married fund-raising and social media tools to on-the-ground screenings. Today, the site is a hub for promotion, sales, and event coordination around a range of politically tinged documentaries, including Moore's 2008 election-related effort, *Slacker Uprising*.

The film also offered BNF producers a chance to experiment with short online video. YouTube, which had launched officially in October 2005, offered an unprecedented chance for rapid response and viral activism. "We are not just content to sit back and try to grow our e-mail list," Sarah Feeley, the company's production head, told the *Chicago Tribune* in September 2006. "The landscape's changed tremendously," she says. "The advent of YouTube has completely changed the playing field."[22]

2006–8: RETOOLING FOR VIRAL VIDEO

At a September 2008 symposium at the Park Center for Independent Media in Ithaca, New York, Greenwald explained that when BNF first turned to viral videos, they predicted a million and a half views within their first year. Greenwald said they reached eleven million views in that launch year, and as of September 2008, more than thirty million total views.

"It happens because we have distribution and marketing," said Greenwald at the symposium. "But mainly it happens because people spread them around. Think about that for a minute, the difference in impact. You're sitting at home and some television commercial is on and all you're doing is fast-forwarding to get through it . . . versus somebody that you know forwards an e-mail to you with a video. Right out of the gate, we're so far ahead in terms of impact, that I think that in years to come, we'll look back at the TV as the dinosaur you're running to get away from vs. trusted messengers, people who are sending you videos." The short films made to activate the troops make no bones about the fact that they are activist tools. They resemble political ads and directly mock politicians with no time wasted for cinematic niceties.

"When we think about what kind of projects we take on, it's not about creating eyeballs . . . it's about getting people to do things and get action," says Brave New Films communications director Leighton Woodhouse, who previously worked as an organizer for SEIU. He explains that they create media campaigns around issues that need to be in the news. "The difference between us and other organizations that occupy the same space is that other organizations follow the headlines and take on issues that are already on CNN and in the front page of the *New York Times* . . . we consciously don't pursue those issues. If they're already in the headlines, we don't feel like we have a lot of value to add."

As an example, Woodhouse cites the "War on Greed" campaign, a series of short films focusing on private equity firms, which buy and reorganize companies for their own profit to the detriment of workers and taxpayers.[23] The series focused on Henry Kravis, a founder of buyout company Kohlberg Kravis Roberts. It premiered in December 2007, during a protest outside of Roberts's Park Avenue home, playing on sandwich boards outfitted with flat-screen TVs. The PR stunt sparked humorous coverage in the *New Yorker*, and Greenwald debated a spokesperson for the private equity industry on CNBC's show *Closing Bell.*[24]

Other short video campaigns have targeted Rudy Giuliani's presidential campaign, the dissembling of Attorney General Alberto Gonzales around the firings of U.S. attorneys, and "The REAL McCain," which pounced on misstatements by the presidential candidate and mocked his policy positions. Each campaign is tied to tools for action: petitions, contact information, other suggestions. According to Woodhouse, the short videos have allowed BNF to both respond immediately to the news cycle and to work with partners to "engage in a dialogue" with their target. The goal is to "bubble the stuff up and get it into mainstream media outlets."

In the case of Fox News, what began as a single film morphed into a persistent campaign—a series of videos on different topics organized under the label "Fox Attacks." One video, accompanied by a suggestive voice-over that mocks late-night phone chat commercials, examines the news channel's salacious use of pornographic footage under the guise of moral outrage over exploitation of women.[25] Fox Attacks urged viewers to lodge protests with Fox advertisers and to sign a pledge not to watch the channel; more than 25,000 people signed a related petition calling for "à la carte" cable television (giving them the ability to exclude Fox from their cable package). Other videos dissected Fox's positions on liberal bloggers, the environment, the Bush administration's plans to invade Iran, and racist attacks against Barack Obama during the presidential campaign.

The Fox Attacks Web site brings it all together: a blog, the videos, fact sheets, viral tools, and a coalition of partners, including Media Matters, Free Press, MoveOn, NewsHounds, Democrats.com, AfterDowningStreet, Democracy for America, DontAttack-Iran.org, Sierra Club, Color of Change, Progressive Christians Uniting, Velvet Revolution.us, and Justice Through Music.[26]

A major hit of the 2008 campaign season came along when Brave New Films teamed up with the AFL-CIO and SEIU to release a four-minute video titled "McCain's Mansions" on August 18 as part of its ongoing series "The Real McCain." At the time, the Obama and McCain campaigns were neck and neck, and many Obama supporters were grumbling that Obama was not hitting McCain hard enough. But what was to be the bombshell?

Brave New Films producers sniffed out a potential opportunity to slam McCain on his repeated characterizations of Obama as an elitist after reading a few online items from blogs such as the Huffington Post about the number of houses McCain owned. While the story had been reported on in different progressive blogs, it had received no pickup from the mainstream media. Instead of letting the story go, BNF released "McCain's Mansions," which interspersed shots of a number of McCain's houses and their price tags (ranging from $850,000 to over $4 million) with clips from an interview with Eileen Gills, a woman who had lost her home.[27]

Not long after the video hit the Huffington Post and Daily Kos, *Politico* reporters Jonathan Martin and Mike Allen asked McCain how many houses he owned. McCain's infamous answer, "I'll have my staff get back to you," incited a tidal wave of derision from the media, late-night comedians, the Obama campaign, and the general American populace. By early October, the YouTube clip had more than half a million views.

The video directly challenged McCain's messages around the economy and also moved mainstream reporters, who had long been fans of the supposed maverick, to make a deeper critique of the Republican senator. BNF's innovations complemented those of the Obama strategists; on October 7 the campaign posted a documentary online about McCain's relationship to Charles Keating, a central figure in the savings and loan scandal.[28]

As the release of "McCain's Mansions" suggests, partnerships with both existing progressive organizations and the netroots have been central to the success of BNF productions. Greenwald has taken an increasingly democratic approach to filmmaking: in addition to harnessing viewers as a new distribution channel and soliciting viewers' support for productions, he has invited them in as collaborators. The NewsHounds are a case in point.[29] For *Outfoxed*, eight MoveOn members volunteered to monitor Fox News to mine damning clips. The effort spun off into its own NewsHounds blog, still faithfully tracking Fox's worst moments four years later.

AMPING UP THE ARMS RACE

Like Greenwald, Cenk Uygur, host of the long-running daily radio and online show *The Young Turks*, has spent the past several years forging his own idiosyncratic media path. A former conservative who graduated from both the Wharton School of Business and Columbia University's Law School, Uygur didn't set out to be a progressive pundit. He says he started *The Young Turks* with his friend Ben Mankowitz in 2002 as "a fun show about current events." By early 2003, it began to bother him that few media commentators were openly criticizing the war. "The less other people talked about it, the more I wanted to scream about it," he said. "The further we got into the Bush administration, the more I became progressive."

As the show became more openly partisan, it was moved to a weekday slot on the satellite radio channel Sirius Left. Uygur and Mankowitz tried to resell it as a weekend show to local analog broadcast stations but had limited success. They found that the talk radio circuit was dominated by conservative hosts and call-in shows, which dictated the choices made by station producers. Eventually, the show was picked up by progressive radio network Air America. In early 2005, at the prompting of Gilliam, they started a live Web show called *The Young Turks*. Uygur often claims the show was the first live, daily Internet TV show.

After setting up a YouTube channel in 2007, *The Young Turks* signed an advertising deal with the video-hosting site and a complementary deal with AOL. The combination of online ad revenue, payments for blogging on AOL, and Web site memberships allowed *The Young Turks* team to quit Air America and call its own shots. Along the way, Uygur became the driving force behind the show—he has gained and lost co-hosts, as well as contracts with Air America and satellite radio, but always retained the *The Young Turks* brand. But no matter the obstacles, he continued to focus on its online show. "Before, you had to beg someone to put you on the air," he said. "In this model, you create your own air. We're broadcasting because we say we are."

Part of the show's success has been its casual mixing of talk, pop culture, and serious politics. "Most people don't just talk about sports or politics or Britney Spears—they talk about all of those things and they have a conversation about it," says Uygur. "People in the younger demographic don't like people reading a prompter and being dispassionate—I'm the opposite, I'm passionate."

That passion pays off. In mid-November 2008, *The Young Turks* announced that they had hit fifty million YouTube views, which they calculate was more than double what McCain did on YouTube over the entire election season.

The successes of BNF and *The Young Turks* lies not just in telling audiences stories but also in inviting audiences to tell their own stories, in addition to helping fund, shape, inform, and distribute the narrative. Fans of *The Young Turks* have been central to expanding its popularity. As Simon Owens reported on the PBS MediaShift site in September, listeners such as A.J. Wysocki, twenty-seven, can serve as "Web soldiers"—promoting the show's content on social media aggregation sites such as Digg.[30] Like the News Hounds, Wysocki has become part of the extended team. Traditional news organizations could never command such loyalty or action.

Furthermore, no old-school objectivity is required or expected. In a September 2008 interview, Greenwald noted, "There's a great line about democracy not being a spectator sport. If you believe that, then the opportunity to take one's storytelling skills and use them around critical issues is quite extraordinary. I love working in film, TV, video, digital and telling stories. Now, telling those stories potentially has an impact on people's lives and issues."

Fighting the right has become a signature—and sometimes even profitable—endeavor for progressive media makers seeking to influence the national conversation. But the new tools for networked communication have also powered an equally important trend: what we call "twenty-first-century muckraking," profiled in the next chapter.

6
EMBRACE TWENTY-FIRST-CENTURY MUCKRAKING

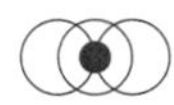

It was a big news week: Hillary Clinton and Barack Obama were gearing up for the presidential race, the iPhone had just been released, and President Bush had just announced a troop surge in Iraq. But the latest startling revelation was just bubbling to the surface—and it came from an unorthodox source.

"Let's extrapolate, shall we? [U. S. Attorney Carol Lam] is on to something that is going to cause a deafening noise," noted commenter "oldtree" on January 13, 2007, on Talking Points Memo (TPM).[1] Oldtree (an online alias) was weighing in at the beginning of what would become a major TPM investigation: the firing of multiple U. S. attorneys around the country for partisan reasons.

Such dialogue has become business as usual at TPM, a news site that has evolved to deftly combine blogging, investigative journalism, and user interaction. TPM not only became the bane of the Republicans during the right's eight-year reign but also kick-started a journalism model that many other media makers admired and sought to emulate.

The moment was ripe for TPM to usher in a dynamic evolution of twenty-first-century muckraking. The volatile ecology for investigative reporting between 2004 and 2008 inspired a number of media experiments with for-profit, nonprofit, and user-driven funding models. Some outlets claimed to be nonpartisan, while others positioned themselves as a corrective to mainstream sources or explicitly described themselves as politically progressive. All were responding to disruptions in old business models for reporting—a crisis that accelerated during Bush's final years in office.

STRATEGIC OPPORTUNITIES

Investigative reporting has long been a tradition for independent print outlets. Progressive magazines such as *Mother Jones* and *The Nation* still have deep commitments to a form of muckraking that prioritizes rigorous reporting, solid fact-checking, and multiple sources, while still seeking to correct social injustices.

In general, conservative outlets don't have a strong investigative tradition. Progressive muckraking tends to focus on corporate and government corruption, uncovering neglect, abuses, and violations of human rights. Sometimes it shades into "oppo research," digging up dirt on political opponents with an eye toward discrediting or unseating them. Investigative reporters may also work closely with grassroots and advocacy groups, or turn an unpopular eye on the internal politics of progressive movements and institutions, revealing the seamier details behind idealistic claims. Progressive journalists are often well ahead of the pack on issues that have particular political resonance for their readers, generating revelations and new leads that mainstream journalists can catch up with days, months, or even years later. The value and leverage of reporting by small media outlets and independent journalists has increased as investigative reporting becomes ever more accessible online, and as mainstream outlets have sliced or disbanded investigative teams altogether.

Credibility is a key issue in the success of high-impact investigative reporting. Progressive outlets are often attacked as unreliable, but muckraking is not by definition partisan. The Pulitzer and Polk awards (among others) have long recognized journalistic enterprise that watchdogs corporations, government, or both. Meanwhile, magazines such as the *New Yorker*, which don't adhere to an explicit ideological slant, provided some of the most influential reporting about the dealings of the Bush administration—most notably stories by veteran investigative reporter Seymour Hersh that revealed shocking conditions at the military prison Abu Ghraib, loosening of existing human rights laws on military torture, and clandestine military operations and plans against Iran.[2]

Overall, investigative reporting units have been robbed of resources, making progressive outlets a final refuge for reporters trained in the craft. In 2008 and into 2009, the outcry related to the "death of journalism" had hit a fever pitch. Americans watched as daily newspapers began to disappear or else cut their print editions and reporting budgets. But this was just the culmination of a decades-long trend. In 2008, renowned investigative reporter Charles Lewis founded American University's Investigative Reporting Workshop in an effort to examine new muckraking models. He notes that before the newspaper crisis became evident to the public, media corporations had dramatically slashed editorial budgets and retired talented reporters and editors early, all in the name of keeping investors happy.

"The net result of this hollowing out process: There are fewer people today to report, write and edit original news stories about our infinitely more complex, dynamic world, . . . important subjects desperately requiring responsible investigation and public education simply go unaddressed," writes Lewis. "When that happens, the public is not as well informed as it could be, important truths do not emerge in a timely, relevant fashion or at all, and accountability of those in power essential to any democracy does not occur."[3]

But at TPM and other outlets we describe in this chapter, the import and influence of investigative journalism aren't disappearing. It is just beginning to look radically different. With this evolution arise new methods and models for affecting the country's political discourse.

For example, for legacy print outlets, investigators would have assembled the pieces of a long feature through extensive quotes, multiple pages, and thousands of words. Now there are options for gathering and rolling out stories in smaller chunks, through blogs, online video, crowd-sourced interaction with users, and more.[4] Long-form articles might be just one iteration of a multiplatform package that includes relevant documents and related links that offer broader and deeper contextualization. The advent of new online visual and interactive elements—including maps, grids, statistics, time lines, discussion boards, searchable databases, and more—can be used to repackage a critical investigative piece for either more expansive or targeted groups of users. Such interfaces might attract audiences who aren't inclined to consume the text of an entire feature-length story.

The gap left by mainstream media has allowed both legacy and emerging progressive outlets to make an impact by experimenting with new reporting and dissemination tools. And these shifts have also provided citizen journalists new opportunities and range to tell their own stories. Thousands of individuals are adding their own perspectives and experience to this new media ecosystem, adapting traditional journalism practices in the process. As this trend matures and these users find their feet, their impact will continue to build. This represents a critical opportunity for existing outlets to integrate users into their own reporting and outreach.

Fostered and managed well, hybridized forms of top-down reporting and organized citizen journalism can cover more ground on key issues of concern to diverse audiences, resulting in more expansive, nuanced, in-depth, and high-impact investigative journalism.

FILLING THE VOID

TPM's innovative news model is driven by founder Joshua Micah Marshall, who has made a career out of reinventing both himself and journalism. A *Columbia Journalism Review* (*CJR*) profile, "The (Josh) Marshall Plan," offers a behind-the-scenes look.

"With his restless institution-building," writes *CJR*'s David Glenn, "he has made as good a case as anyone for blogging's journalistic merits." While attending graduate school at Brown, Marshall realized he would rather write for political magazines than pursue a career in academia. He started TPM in response to the Florida recount debacle while he was working at progressive policy magazine the *American Prospect*, where he served as its Washington editor from 1999 until he quit in 2001. He freelanced for various outlets, online and in print, including *Salon*, *Slate*, and the *Washington Monthly*, maintaining TPM all the while.

TPM hit the national radar with its reporting of Senator Trent Lott's (R-Miss.) remarks at Strom Thurmond's one-hundredth-birthday party. Lott's comments seemed to indicate support for the racist segregationist policies that lost Thurmond the 1948 presidential campaign.

"I want to say this about my state: When Strom Thurmond ran for president, we voted for him," said Lott. "We're proud of it. And if the rest of the country had followed our lead, we wouldn't have had all these problems over all these years, either." [5] TPM uncovered Lott's history of actively supporting segregation during his college days and making similar statements at various points throughout his career, pushing the story with pointed posts such as, "We knew what he meant." [6] TPM doggedly followed the story, although the mainstream media showed little initial interest. Lott was forced to step down from his position as Senate majority leader.

By 2004, Marshall had pieced together enough income from reader contributions and online advertising to devote himself to the site full-time. In the *CJR* piece, Marshall credits Blogads

.com—a site that drives advertisers to packages of niche blogs, including the Liberal Blog Advertising Network—for his chance to make a go of it.[7]

By 2005, the site was growing at a rapid clip. Marshall knew that he could no longer go it alone and needed to add to the TPM masthead. The previous year, Marshall had placed a call out to readers asking for financial support to cover the New Hampshire primary. He was surprised by the response of his audience, which contributed almost $7,000. With this lesson in online fund-raising Marshall went back to his readers and asked them for help in hiring two additional reporters. He ended up raising just over $100,000 to create the companion site, TPMMuckraker.

"This isn't in contributions of $5,000; this is people sending in $10, $25, maybe $50—the occasional $100 and $250," says Marshall. "But certainly 90–95 percent was $50 and under. That basically gave me the money to build the site, rent an office and hire two reporters for a year. My expectation—that proved to be true—was that after a year, it would grow enough that we could sustain it through advertising."[8]

TPM and its sister site, TPMMuckraker, first stumbled across the U.S. attorneys story in the course of a different investigation. Marshall and team had been following the colorful Randall "Duke" Cunningham (R-Calif.) scandal since it broke in mid-2005. The scandal revolved around Representative Cunningham's acceptance of bribes in return for millions of dollars in defense contracts, which he brokered through his position on the Defense Appropriations Subcommittee. Along the way, he made a few shady real estate deals, received gifts of antiques and Jimmy Buffet tickets,[9] and entertained women while dressed in his pajamas on a lava-lamp-lit yacht.[10] Ultimately, Cunningham pled guilty to accepting more than $2.4 million in payoffs and was sentenced to eight years in prison.[11]

On January 12, 2007, while following up on the Cunningham case, TPMMuckracker reporter Justin Rood noted a story from the *San Diego Union-Tribune* detailing how Carol Lam, the U.S. attorney whose office prosecuted Cunningham, had been forced to resign.

"According to this morning's *San Diego Union-Tribune*, the White House's reason for giving her the axe is that she 'failed to make smuggling and gun cases a top priority,'" wrote Rood. "But most folks the paper talked to—supporters and detractors—said that sounded like a load of hooey." Rood also noted a quote from Senator Dianne Feinstein (D-Calif.), who told the paper in a statement, "We don't know how many U.S. Attorneys have been asked to resign—it could be two, it could be ten, it could be more. No one knows."[12]

"We had been reporting on these cases for over a year," noted Marshall in an April 2007 interview on the PBS television show *Bill Moyers Journal*. "That gave us a context to understand what was happening."[13] They put the word out on the firings, and started getting tips from readers.

Throughout mid-January 2007, Marshall, along with TPM-Muckraker staffers Rood and Paul Kiel, and TPM's community of users, kept tabs on the developing scandal. Speculations swirled on the site as users suggested that various U.S. attorneys had been ousted to make room for Bush loyalists, or else because attorneys such as Lam and Nevada's Daniel Bogden were angering the Bush White House. While TPM kept the reporting pressure on, inside-the-Beltway press dismissed their efforts. "Some liberals are seeing broad partisan conspiracies where none likely exist," wrote *Time*'s Jay Carney.[14]

Carney and his cohort were soon proven wrong. As they initiated their own investigation, TPM reporters also kept close tabs on stories from local newspapers related to U.S. attorney firings. In addition to Lam, seven others were removed: Bogden, Paul Charlton (Arizona), Margaret Chiara (western Michigan), H.E. "Bud" Cummins III (eastern Arkansas), David Iglesias (New Mexico),

John McKay (western Washington), and Kevin Ryan (northern California). What was common to all eight individuals? They were either focusing too closely on the questionable activities of Bush administration officials—including the extent of CIA executive director Kyle "Dusty" Foggo's communication with the president about illegal torture conducted by CIA operatives—or refusing to give in to political demands made by Republicans. With behind-the-scenes help from readers, TPM writers also uncovered evidence that Republicans were installing overtly partisan U.S. attorneys in key swing states just in time for the 2008 race.[15]

As Marshall noted in a September 8, 2008, speech, all the elements came together to set the stage for success. "The particular advantage that our readers gave us was a really big deal. And I'd seen enough up to that point—when [the Bush administration's] argument was that they [coincidentally] happened to fire eight U.S. attorneys—that made me more persistent. So it's a matter of stories we were covering, a very deep level of skepticism we had about the people we were covering, and the neat advantages of our relationship with our readers," he said.[16]

By piecing together different strands over several months, TPM was able to scoop mainstream journalism outlets on the story. As Senator John Kerry told the *Financial Times*, he'd call Marshall a "progressive Matt Drudge in the ascendancy, but Josh actually does the journalistic spadework."[17] Best of all, the investigation yielded results. Following extended congressional investigations, two top Justice Department officials, Michael Battle and Kyle Sampson, resigned. Attorney General Alberto Gonzales, who had overseen the staff that authorized the firings, resigned months later.

By October 2007, TPM had certainly appeared on the Bush administration's radar. A January 2008 post by Kiel noted that the media outlet had been scrubbed from the Department of Justice's (DOJ) press release list.[18] The DOJ denied any retaliatory motive, replying, "As you may realize we have a lot of requests to be put on our media lists and we simply are not able to put everyone on the list." In a February 7 hearing, Representative John Conyers Jr. (D-Mich.) asked Attorney General Michael Mukasey why TPM was removed from the list.[19] Mukasey later explained that the rationale was that TPM lacked "credentials." Notably, TPM began receiving DOJ press releases again in late February.[20]

CULTIVATING THE BEST POSSIBLE IN-BOX

By 2008, Talking Points Memo and its sister sites had an average of 1.5 million readers a month, topping out at three million during the election season. According to deputy publisher Andrew Golis, during that time TPM received an average of a thousand e-mails a day from readers who were passing along tips, commenting on articles, or engaging in ongoing political conversations with Marshall and his staff. While many media outlets are similarly overwhelmed by reader correspondence, what sets TPM apart is how they manage the influx. Golis noted that all staff are required to read e-mails and respond as much as they can.

Golis says the strategy is to treat the audience like sources: "We want to cultivate the best possible in-box." TPM staff feed yet more contributions by acknowledging tips and conversations from their e-mail correspondence on the news site.

Writing for the *New Yorker* in March 2008, Eric Alterman noted that Marshall hadn't originally planned to incorporate user involvement in his work.[21] However, Marshall's willingness to look beyond the "professional sources" favored by mainstream reporters for quick sound bites and user-friendly quotes allowed him to glean information from readers more directly involved in the issues at hand, such as government weather trackers who offered up details on the Katrina debacle.

In an April 2005 post to his readers, Marshall celebrated this evolving method, terming it "open-source muck-raking." The post corresponded with an announcement that TPM would be adding a companion site that would feature a group blog and a forum for readers to "raise and hash out questions," and discuss issues:

> When people guest-blog on TPM, they never fail to be amazed at just how much quality information comes in from readers. And in this case, I don't just mean solid thinking and analysis, but concrete factual data. It would have been impossible for me, for instance, to have written most of what I've written on Social Security over the last few months if I didn't have literally thousands of people reading their local papers and letting me know what they're seeing or reporting back from town hall meetings or giving me the heads up on things that are about to break on the hill. That's not a replacement for journalism; it's different. But it's potentially very powerful. . . . Many of you have been sending in tips for months, contacting representatives and senators, sending in news stories that aren't getting picked up in the national press. We're looking for ways to put you [in touch] with each other more directly, to facilitate that sort of exchange or activism on others issues beside Social Security."[22]

As Marshall told Moyers, "One of the unique strengths of our journalism model is that we use our readers a lot to [do] the front line research for us. That doesn't mean we just take things people say and print them willy-nilly. But, there's a wealth of information out there in small metropolitan papers around the country. So, there were reports about the Arkansas U.S. Attorney who had been fired, that was just in [local] Arkansas media. And there was another similar case with the U.S. Attorney in Michigan."[23]

This reliance on aggregation and linking may irk the small-town mainstream reporters who do the legwork, but it's tailor-made for the online news environment. Small and dogged, TPM served as a lens to focus sustained attention on the scandal in a way that most mainstream news outlets are not prepared—much less interested—to do.

ASSESSING TPM'S IMPACT

Even by conventional impact measurements, TPM has achieved notable success. The site won the 2008 George Polk Award for Legal Reporting around the U.S. attorneys scandal—becoming the first Web-only news site to do so. At various points the site has led the charge on stories about Valerie Plame's unmasking, Jack Abramoff's lobbying scandals, and Bush's attempt to privatize Social Security.

Marshall's tone is often casual, and he is progressive in his coverage. By openly declaring his political views, Marshall suggests, he is offering readers transparency that they won't find at mainstream media outlets that claim to be objective.

Marshall has not only shifted the paradigm for twenty-first-century muckraking. Under his guidance, the site's blog model has evolved and matured over the years, growing from a single-contributor blog into a for-profit LLC with donor, ad, and video revenue. TPM Café, which was launched in May 2005, features blogs about domestic and foreign policy issues by academics, journalists, and former public officials, among others, as well as an influential online book club where political books are debated.

In a November 2008 post Marshall laid out TPM's postelection strategy. He noted that each two-year election cycle had spurred organizational changes, but posited that this one would offer a fresh start:

> I think it's important to step back to recognize just how new it is in the history of the country. On paper, there was last

> unified Democratic control in Washington sixteen years ago during President Clinton's first two years in office and before that during President Carter's presidency. Looks, however, are deceiving. For more than half a century before 1992, the Democratic party was actually two parties, even after the Civil Rights movement cleared the old-style segregationists and neo-dixiecrats from the party—a national party and a southern one, a fact that created conservative governing majorities on numerous issues. What's more, both Clinton and Carter ran on platforms of bucking their party and its entrenched congressional majorities. For both these reasons and many others, what will begin in January is something this country hasn't really seen since the first half of the 20th century.
>
> So January will usher in a new Democratic Ascendancy in Washington. And here at TPM we believe we are uniquely qualified to chronicle it. So to that end we are hiring two new reporter-bloggers to be based in Washington, DC, one assigned to the White House and one assigned to Capitol Hill. The Obama White House and the expanded Democratic majorities on Capitol Hill are unquestionably the political story of the next two years. And with your help we plan to be there on the ground and here in New York, covering it in force, fully, critically and down to the minute.[24]

Marshall chose to hire Matthew Cooper—a former reporter for *Time* and *Newsweek* who faced threats of jail for refusing to reveal sources related to the Valerie Plame case—to become the site's editor at large. "This just in from the Department of Good Gets," opined Megan Garber on the *CJR* blog:

> The Cooper-Marshall union seems to be [a] kind of symbiotically charged coup. . . . [T]he Web-based news operation

> validated by the name-brand, traditional-media-oriented journalist; that journalist, in turn, validated by the name-brand, non-traditional outlet. The organization gets clout; the journalist gets freedom (and the distinction of being "forward thinking" in his approach to journalism). If Cooper's hiring at TPM ends up being that kind of win-win . . . it could actually end up as a win-win-win. Because there's another group that tends to benefit from this merging of traditional and new media: readers.[25]

MUCKRAKING ON THE MOVE

TPM offers one model that many will emulate, and the site itself continues to evolve. But it is not the only reporting model that's shaking things up.

American University's Lewis suggests that hybrid journalism projects, such as reporting centers based at universities, could provide an infusion of cash and talent into investigative projects. Such centers would decouple reporting from particular news outlets, instead offering the results of investigations online and for redistribution among multiple outlets, much like syndicated news services, but with more resources dedicated to deep investigation. The Center for Public Integrity, which Lewis founded in 1989 and left in 2005, follows this model.

Such projects are more accessible in an online environment shaped by search, linking, and referrals rather than by print/broadcast-dominant media brands. One significant consequence of the online convergence of many news outlets—small and large; print, audio, and video—has been that news broken by citizen journalists or independent outlets has the potential to make as large a splash as stories by big national media. In the 24/7 cycle, breaking scoops are immediately spread, dissected, amplified, and republished, offering continual openings for reporters whose work might never have seen the light in the analog era. On the flip side, the roar of information can drown out even the most scandalous and meticulously researched story.

Mother Jones successfully capitalized on popular interest in the election by opening a Washington bureau in late 2007, hiring noted journalist David Corn away from *The Nation* to head it. Throughout the last few years, *Mother Jones* has stayed true to its reporter-led investigative-reporting roots with much success. In 2008, the media outlet won the National Magazine Award for General Excellence. Under Corn and its D.C. bureau team, the magazine snagged a number of scoops, including revelations about the prominent role that McCain advisor Phil Gramm played in the deregulation that contributed to the financial meltdown,[26] and the unmasking of Mary Lou Sapone, a mole on the NRA's payroll who infiltrated three gun control organizations. These stories spawned a variety of follow-ups in mainstream outlets, from the *Washington Post* to the Associated Press to *Good Morning America*, and even the conservative *Washington Times* and *National Review* covered the Gramm flap. MSNBC anchor Keith Olbermann added Sapone to his notorious "Worst Person in the World" list, and Senator Frank Lautenberg of New Jersey wrote a public letter to the NRA demanding an explanation.

Mother Jones regularly supplements its traditional print coverage with online extras, including "Lie by Lie," a popular interactive time line that tracks the history of the Iraq war from 1990 to 2008.[27] Such visual repositories offer deep wells of data for researchers and bloggers alike and provide opportunities to repurpose news pieces and investigations that might quickly disappear. What these online extras haven't provided, however, is a genuinely participatory opportunity for users to contribute their own analysis or corrections.

At a 2009 Netroots Nation–sponsored event in San Francisco, co-editor Clara Jeffery expressed her ongoing skepticism about new models in reporting. "What I'm worried about is the loss of coverage of local politics, board meetings, and only a few newspapers have a sustained presence in Iraq. There are some bloggers there and freelancers, but they can't tell the story the same way that a large news organization can. I'm not convinced that the decentralized model can work, and provide all the resources for copy editing and fact checking."[28]

But *Mother Jones* is looking to embrace the networked media landscape, recognizing the need to cultivate an online active community. In 2009, Mother Jones debuted a new Web site with this goal in mind. According to a March 2009 interview with Knight Pulse, Nick Aster (*Mother Jones*'s "media architect") noted that the redesign was focused on providing more space for their community to identify solutions and elicit reactions, interact with each other, and organize themselves.

Aster said *Mother Jones* hoped to "see action that took place by virtue of our journalism [with] a tangible result that we can point to and say 'Wow, that actually led to that.'"[29]

THE POWER AND PITFALLS OF CROWD-SOURCING

One of the most successful crowd-sourcing experiments in this period was Off the Bus (OTB), a citizen journalism project launched in July 2007 on the Huffington Post in partnership with New York University professor Jay Rosen, a longtime proponent of "pro-am" (professional-amateur) or citizen journalism. The partnership was a success. By October 2008, more than five million people had visited OTB's Web site to read its coverage.

Off the Bus was designed to break the traditional, top-down "reporting" mold and involve participants more deeply and authentically in politics. "There's a lot of civic education involved." Rosen said in an interview with us at the 2007 Yearly Kos conference. "It's a way of increasing participation in the election, which

I think is a good thing. I believe democracy is a participatory sport."

Inspired by Timothy Crouse's 1973 account of campaign reporting, *The Boys on the Bus*, the project was designed to harness the labor, passion, and expertise of contributors who weren't part of the professional press corps trailing the candidates. Participants could contribute in a variety of ways: through crowd-sourced reporting projects, blogging, or serving as experts on call for other OTB reporters. Rosen's hedging about the political aims of the project in a July 2007 conversation with journalism professor Leonard Witt demonstrates the charged discussion about media bias in muckraking 2.0:

> Let me quote from our About page, which I wrote: "The site covers the campaigns of all the candidates for president in both parties. It is independent and unaffiliated with either the Democratic or Republican Party. Its perspective is determined by the publishers, Arianna Huffington and Jay Rosen; by the editorial staff they hire, and by individual authors and producers who use our platform. There is no party line."
>
> But we also do not deny: I have a political identity, so does Arianna, as will our contributors. We are not going into the "objective journalism" biz. . . . I am not worried about what bin you toss the resulting work into. I am worried about whether it is good, relevant to the campaign, and whether it reveals the world well and attracts a following on the Web.[30]

Rosen explains that he was applying lessons learned from a previous crowd-sourcing experiment, NewAssignment.net—which was designed as an innovation lab to experiment with new journalism models including citizen journalism and crowd-sourcing. Rosen notes that working with volunteers is tricky and labor-intensive.

"You have to be very clear about what you're expecting people to do," he says, and it's important to divide labor "in a way that connects to people's motivations for joining the project." Volunteers need to know the task at hand, how it fits into the larger project, and what the expected impact is.

Off the Bus hired Amanda Michel, who had worked with the Dean and Kerry-Edwards campaigns as an organizer, to navigate this tricky terrain. "The campaign *is* the journalism," said Rosen. But instead of asking their users for money, they were asking them for attention, blog posts, and research.

In contrast, Rosen criticizes legacy progressive media as elitist and closed. "The progressive media sphere is surprisingly professionalized. It is very much stuck in an elite-masses model, and it had, over a period of time from around counterculture to present, developed a structure and a class of people who liked running these progressive media organizations. . . . There is this long tradition of mobilizing the masses on the left, the notion of a vanguard which leads, and if necessary, manipulates the masses for the greater good."

By partnering with Huffington Post, OTB acquired a built-in community and a vehicle for visibility. Many times, OTB contributors landed on HuffPo's front page, alongside links to *New York Times* pieces. The reporting project differentiated itself from opinion-based political blogging by encouraging contributors to pick a beat and uncover new information or make new connections. The hope was that citizen reporters would be less jaded and more independent than the professional journalists granted inside access by the campaigns.

"Even this early in the process, we've already seen example after example of what happens when reporters hop on board the same bus—and the Conventional Wisdom gets passed around like a joint at a Grateful Dead concert," wrote Arianna Huffington in a post announcing the project's launch. "And we've also seen far-too-much coverage in which it becomes hard to tell where the campaigns' agendas leave off and the journalists' reporting kicks in."[31]

Off the Bus staff worked hard to not talk down to users, and as a result, it gained both active participation and eyeballs. Once again the *Columbia Journalism Review* was on the case. Michel offered a retrospective on the project in the March/April 2009 issue:

> Collectively, we could do what a single reporter or traditional news organization could not. We dispatched people to report on dozens of events happening simultaneously around the country. We distributed research tasks among hundreds of volunteers, instead of a handful of paid reporters working full-time for weeks. Ground-level access, networked intelligence, and distributed labor became our editorial mainstays. More than twelve thousand people eventually signed up to participate in one way or another, including seventeen hundred writers. With such numbers, Mayhill Fowler's Bittergate story—or something like it—was almost inevitable.
>
> It sounds impressive: twelve thousand people. But the challenge was not persuading them to sign up. It was figuring out what they were willing and able to do after that, and then cost-effectively coordinating their efforts so that they added up to real journalism. By Election Day, we had solved enough of that puzzle that I can now say to professional journalists: we found a viable pro-am model for advancing stories both around the globe and in your backyards, and you should take a serious look at it.[32]

Raise your hand if you understand Michel's "Bittergate" reference. This tsunami of a story almost washed out the Obama campaign when Mayhill Fowler, a sixty-one-year-old OTB volunteer, captured and reported on a controversial Obama quote at a private fund-raiser in April 2008:

> You go into some of these small towns in Pennsylvania, and like a lot of small towns in the Midwest, the jobs have been gone now for 25 years and nothing's replaced them. And they fell through the Clinton Administration, and the Bush Administration, and each successive administration has said that somehow these communities are gonna regenerate and they have not. And it's not surprising then they get bitter, they cling to guns or religion or antipathy to people who aren't like them or anti-immigrant sentiment or anti-trade sentiment as a way to explain their frustrations.[33]

The quote itself was instant fodder for conservatives hoping to paint Obama as an elitist liberal and for mainstream pundits to rally around a new scandal. But that was not the only driver of the story. Fowler herself came under scrutiny.

"This is where citizen-journalism gets very fuzzy," wrote Michael Tomasky, the editor at large of the Web site *Guardian American* and former editor of the *American Prospect*, noting that Fowler had gained access to the dinner as an Obama donor, not a citizen reporter. By traditional journalistic rules, Obama's comment would have been off the record. "Now isn't that a convenient definition of citizen-journalist?" chided Tomasky. "Put on a citizen hat, and donate enough money to be sure that you get invited into private affairs as a citizen—something no journalist I know would do. Then, once inside the door, put on the journalist hat and report private remarks! And finally, to absolve yourself of the standard journalistic responsibility of going to aides and getting on-the-record quotes about the comment, which most any working journalist would do, toss the journalist hat back in the closet and become a citizen again! Nice work if you can get it."[34]

Tomasky's solutions: compel citizen journalists to reveal any political donations, and to seek out clarifications or retorts from the people they quote.

"We're in uncharted territory here," retorted Rosen.

> Descriptor languages missing. People get mad when they don't know what to call things. Mad or daft. . . . Citizen journalism isn't a hypothetical in this campaign. It's not a beach ball for newsroom curmudgeons, either. It's Mayhill Fowler, who had been in Pennsylvania with Obama, listening to the candidate talk about Pennsylvanians to supporters in San Francisco, and hearing something that didn't sound right to her. Who's Mayhill Fowler? A 61-year-old citizen journalist who supports Obama. . . . Fowler is a particular kind of Obama loyalist. The kind with a notebook, a tape recorder, some friends in the campaign, a public platform of decent size, plus the faculty of critical intelligence. The campaign doesn't know what it thinks about such people. But soon the people around the candidates will realize: this is normal.[35]

Rosen described Fowler's boundary-crossing as "a state of mutual chartlessness," but Jeff Jarvis—a social media evangelist and director of the interactive journalism program at City University of New York's Graduate School of Journalism—had a chart for it: the "Press-Sphere" (see page 120). "Tomasky thinks that news happens by journalism's rules and he's upset the rules have changed and wants new rules. But who ever gave journalism hegemony over news?" asked Jarvis. "News is what happens and what people witness and what they can now share, with or without journalists. That's the new rule of the press-sphere: nobody rules." Jarvis suggested that we eliminate the label of "journalist," replacing it with "witness," and prioritizing openness over professional rules of conduct.[36]

Rosen tracked others' responses: Robert Niles at the *Online*

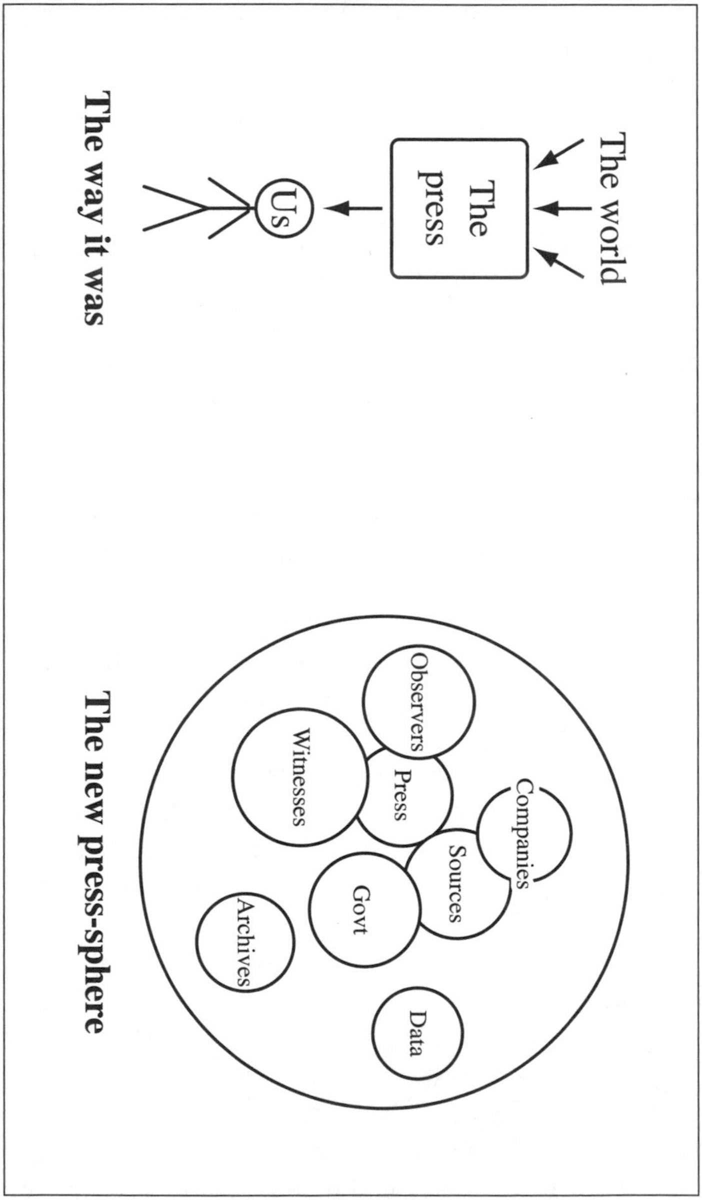

The world

The press

Us

The way it was

Observers

Companies

Witnesses

Press

Sources

Govt

Archives

Data

The new press-sphere

In an April 2008 blog post titled "The Press Becomes the Press-Sphere," CUNY's Jeff Jarvis sketched out his vision of how the journalism environment had transformed in the networked era.

Jeff Jarvis, "The Press Becomes the Press-Sphere," BuzzMachine, April 14, 2008, http://www.buzzmachine.com/2008/04/14/the-press-becomes-the-press-sphere

Journalism Review suggested that "there is no such thing as off the record anymore." Robert Cox of the Media Bloggers Association opined, "The issue is less the distinction between 'citizen' and 'journalist' and more whether the Founding Fathers ever contemplated such a distinction in the first place. A close reading of the First Amendment and centuries of legal precedent says 'no.'" And journalism professor Mindy McAdams warned, "Naming who is a journalist—and who is not—is a dangerous, dangerous course to follow."[37]

Amid the fog of debate, one thing was clear: Off the Bus had made an impact. Not only did Fowler's post generate a hundred thousand hits within a day, it launched a new electoral talking point and significantly challenged journalistic norms.[38] And the project's accomplishments weren't just limited to "gotcha" moments like Bittergate. Michel ticked off a range of reporting efforts in her *CJR* article, from organizing 227 contributors to dig up background details on superdelegates, to assigning a blogger to cover a breaking hostage situation at Hillary Clinton's campaign office in New Hampshire, to sending volunteers out with Obama canvassers to assess on-the-ground reactions to new campaign slogans. A personal report from blogger Wende Marshall about her rising blood pressure led to a HuffPo story about the effect of Obama's campaign on the anxiety levels of African American women. All of this was unpaid, which meant the quality of reporting varied widely.

Michel noted that Off the Bus staff spent most of their time providing editorial guidance, fact-checking, and offering citizen reporters tips of the trade. "Ultimately, many more felt comfortable being impressionistic, profiling their and their friends' experiences around the campaign. They resisted hard leads. We risked becoming the Monet School of Journalism."

She suggested that professional journalists will need to switch from an ethic of neutrality to an ethic of transparency and disclosure in order to work successfully with pro-am reporters. For progressive media, it will require continuing their tradition of combining ideological stances with a commitment to fact-checking and rigorous investigation. "The timing for a new social contract between the press and the public could not be better," Michel concluded. "There will be no reason to mourn the loss of its audience if the press fully understands and exploits the new reality that its audience can now be its ally."

THE BEST OF BOTH WORLDS

While citizen journalism and online tools and platforms are changing the nature of journalism itself, there is still a critical need for well-sourced, highly trained, employed reporters to continue their traditional muckraking. In order for progressive outlets to make an impact, they will need both to adapt new roles and tools and to support long-form, labor-intensive investigation.

Finding the resources to support this will continue to be a challenge, especially for flagging print outlets. By late 2008, a number of experimental models had begun to point the way. Pro Publica, a freestanding investigative newsroom funded by liberal philanthropists Herbert M. and Marion O. Sandler, aimed to produce high-profile investigations and distribute them to national outlets that would create the biggest splash.[39] The Center for Independent Media, a network of state-based investigative news sites, pulled in both trained journalists and bloggers to shore up the reporting failures of local newspapers. And the Spot.us project, founded by David Cohn, former editor of NewAssignment.net, harnessed crowd-sourcing to fund targeted investigations through "community funded reporting."

Like many of their print counterparts, these projects don't claim an explicit progressive mandate, preferring instead to stress transparency, independence, and civic responsibility. In doing so, they vie for funds and buzz with their more ideological peers, described in the previous chapter. But as the next chapter shows, fighting the right and twenty-first-century muckraking can offer powerful synergies when combined to tackle political flash points.

7
TAKE IT TO THE HILL

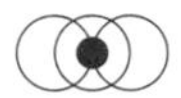

On the morning of October 18, 2007, Adam Green was surfing the Web when he came across a *New York Times* article reporting that Senate Democrats had cut a deal with President Bush "to give telephone carriers legal immunity for any role they played in the National Security Agency's domestic eavesdropping program." This announcement contradicted a statement that Senator (and then presidential candidate) Chris Dodd had made on his blog just the day before: "I will do what I can to see to it that no telecommunications giant that was complicit in this Administration's assault on the Constitution is given a get-out-of-jail-free card."

Green—at the time MoveOn's civic communications director—knew a flash point when he saw one. First, he sent Dodd's post to a cluster of progressive bloggers who had been following the issue: Glenn Greenwald, who founded Unclaimed Territory (later transformed into a regular column on *Salon*); Jane Hamsher of Firedoglake; Markos Moulitsas of Daily Kos; Matt Stoller, now at OpenLeft; and a handful of others. Together they strategized about the best way to hold Dodd's feet to the fire.

Green also fired off a request to MoveOn members, asking, "Can you call Senator Chris Dodd's presidential campaign today? Ask Dodd to announce he'll put a 'hold' on any bill that gives retroactive immunity to law-breaking phone companies." Calls started pouring in, making staffers at Dodd's campaign headquarters feel like they were under siege. The chase was on.

STRATEGIC OPPORTUNITIES

Campaigns designed to affect legislation knit together the different strands of the progressive media network. Reporters dig for tales of pork, malfeasance, corruption, and injustice, making the case for change. The fight-the-right crowd targets opponents to key legislation and counters conservative frames on the issue. Experts and pundits stake out positions on the issue in question across progressive magazines, Web sites, and broadcast outlets.

Legislative campaigns also shift the moneymaking aspects of political communication into high gear. Advocacy groups crank up their direct-mail and e-mail operations, alternately showering voters with calls to action and calls for funding. Lobbyists wine, dine . . . and whine: to Congress, the press, anyone who will listen. Opposing factions purchase ads, call in favors based on campaign donations, usher in grassroots and "Astroturf" allies to cite contradictory claims, and recruit dignitaries to host glittering fundraising dinners. In short, lawmaking is a free-for-all, but rarely a free lunch: too often, advocates have to pay to play. That makes the buzz-building power of networked progressive media—predicated on smart uses of free platforms and the many layers of existing networks—especially valuable.

The work that progressive bloggers, media makers, and activists have done to highlight and affect legislation surrounding warrantless wiretapping created a model for future coalitions to "take it to the Hill." Such coordinated campaigns can determine whether a bill makes it to the president's desk or dies on the House floor.

Legislative battles provide a sharp context for measuring the impact of progressive media projects. Writers, editors, and producers work to craft stories that will reveal injustices, demonstrate the consequences of bad policy, and move both the public and policy makers to act. To succeed, they have to both follow and push the news cycle, laying down the foundation for critique and then pouncing on news hooks as they surface.

Different hubs in the progressive media network can play different roles. Green describes how the overall dynamic developed between 2004 and 2008. "Having a progressive reporter with the ability to ask questions to those in power very much improves the effectiveness of activism, providing accountability, while progressive blogs have the ability to create headlines, which moves beyond the pressure from phone calls."

Green suggests that legacy progressive media can also keep momentum going by writing in depth about policies and legislation when the mainstream outlets have not yet been drawn to the issue. As Bush's popularity waned and new hosts appeared on cable channels, progressive magazines have also begun to provide a stable of talking heads—Katrina vanden Heuvel and Christopher Hayes of *The Nation*; David Corn, now at *Mother Jones*; and talkers from multiple other outlets—to "keep up the drumbeat" about key policy decisions on the Sunday shows and on cable news. Compared to the post-9/11 drought of alternative perspectives on cable news, this was refreshing, although we're still far from parity when it comes to seeing a diversity of perspectives on the 24/7 stations.

Throughout the final years of the Bush administration, the fight over the Foreign Intelligence Surveillance Act (FISA) drew together all levels of the progressive media network: networked individuals, self-organizing networks, networks organized by institutions, and networks of institutions.

It also crossed all platforms. Book publishing played a signal role early on, driving innovation in the networked progressive media sphere along the way. Bloggers were centrally involved in the fight, partnering with online advocates. "If MoveOn didn't have blogs to collaborate with, they would have put a bunch of phone calls into the front desk of a presidential campaign, which would have been noted and ignored. Blogs made the fight more public," says Green.

And more piled on. MSNBC host Keith Olbermann joined in the fray on cable news, regularly reporting on and denouncing administration policies on surveillance, privacy, and telecom amnesty. Naomi Klein and Chris Hedges of the *The Nation* signed on to an ACLU lawsuit challenging illegal surveillance of U.S. citizens, including independent journalists.[1] Then, during the 2008 election, both new and established social networking platforms provided an infusion of citizen media content, commentary, and pressure.

HOW PROGRESSIVE BLOGGERS AND ACTIVISTS AFFECTED THE FIGHT AROUND WARRANTLESS WIRETAPPING

Warrantless wiretapping had long been a sore spot for the left. Congress passed the FISA in 1978, in response to government abuses of surveillance revealed during the Watergate hearings. Surveillance in domestic criminal cases is governed by its own set of laws, but warrants involving international surveillance are regulated at the federal level. For reasons of national security, the law created a secret court, the Foreign Intelligence Surveillance court, to hear government requests for wiretaps designed to ferret out foreign intelligence.[2]

In the wake of 9/11, the Bush administration refused to heed FISA restrictions, using the so-called Patriot Act to expand surveillance activities by the National Security Agency (NSA). In December 2005, the *New York Times* revealed the extent of the government's warrantless wiretapping program.[3] "Under a presidential order signed in 2002, the intelligence agency has monitored the international telephone calls and international e-mail messages of hundreds, perhaps thousands, of people inside the United States without warrants over the past three years in an effort to track possible 'dirty numbers' linked to Al Qaeda," wrote *Times* reporters James Risen and Eric Lichtblau. "The agency, [officials] said, still seeks warrants to monitor entirely domestic communications." Most people targeted for NSA monitoring had never been charged with a crime, making this an unprecedented breach of privacy for Americans. Disturbingly, the article noted that *New York Times* editors had delayed publication of these revelations for a year after requests from the White House to suppress the story for national security reasons.

Intelligence officials argued that the process of obtaining warrants was too cumbersome and would not allow them to root out the terrorists quickly enough. Critics countered that they were breaking the law and threatening civil liberties. What was worse, the wiretapping was only part of a much broader mandate to spy on U. S. citizens via the ominously named Department of Homeland Security.[4]

After pressure from Congress, administration officials promised to pass requests through the FISA court in early 2007. But in July 2007, intelligence officials pushed back, pressuring Congress to pass the Protect America Act, which temporarily lifted FISA restrictions, allowing the warrantless wiretapping to continue. Civil libertarians protested that if Congress succeeded in granting the telecom companies immunity, it would send the signal that the administration's executive overreach was acceptable. They argued that this was a slippery slope, one better handled by the legal system.

Greenwald himself was a civil rights litigator who had left his practice in 2005 to "do other things which I thought were more engaging and could make more of an impact, including political writing."[5] He founded the blog Unclaimed Territory and quickly gained national attention. Greenwald simultaneously functioned as a reporter, an advocate, and a topic-area expert, peppering vigorous analysis with deep background on related legal issues. He broke the scoop that Senator Mike DeWine (R-Ohio) had in 2002 proposed alternative eavesdropping standards that the administration dismissed as unconstitutional.[6] Senator Russ Feingold (D-Wis.) cited the blog in March 2006 when he introduced Senate Resolution 398 to censure the president.[7]

On October 18, 2007, Greenwald wrote on Unclaimed Territory, "The question of whether the telecoms acted in 'good faith' in allowing warrantless government spying on their customers is already pending before a court of law. In fact, that is one of the central issues in the current lawsuits—one that AT&T has already lost in a federal court . . . . Yet that is the issue that [Senators Jay Rockefeller and Mike McConnell]—operating in secret—are taking away from the courts by passing a law declaring the telecoms to have won."[8]

By pressuring Dodd to put a hold on the bill, the bloggers and activists hoped to draw attention to the Democrats' stance on a key civil rights issue that also had legs among independent and libertarian voters. If Senate majority leader Harry Reid of Nevada denied the hold, then Dodd's next move would be to call for a filibuster. But they thought he needed moral support to hold the line. Talking Points Memo's Greg Sargent then stepped into the fray, asking Dodd if he'd take a stand. By 1:55 P.M. on the eighteenth, TPM had the exclusive: Dodd announced that he'd be sending a letter later that day to Harry Reid announcing the hold.[9]

Bloggers rewarded Dodd's courage with a round of praise: Eschaton, Daily Kos, Open Left, MyDD, Firedoglake, Crooks and Liars, Hullaballoo, and America Blog all joined the chorus. "I'm not supporting anyone . . . but I always believe in rewarding good behavior," wrote Atrios of Eschaton.[10] "Dodd has made the preservation of our constitution the centerpiece of his run for the presidency and he's putting himself on the line in the Senate on this one. For that he deserves our gratitude," wrote Digby of Hullaballoo.[11] "Chris Dodd will be literally standing up for us on FISA, and for quite a long time," wrote Chris Bowers of OpenLeft. "He's going to need some help. Both we, and other Senators who oppose retroactive immunity, must stand with him."[12]

Taking a stand paid off for Dodd's campaign that week: the candidate raised $200,000 in the thirty-six hours after announcing the hold, and he leaped from seventh to second in the Daily

Kos presidential straw poll. "There is definitely a Dodd boomlet happening among the netroots," Micah Sifry, co-founder of Tech-President, told *The Nation.*[13] Mainstream reporters also took note. "Here's a first for a Senate presidential candidate," wrote Shailagh Murray on the *Washington Post* campaign diary, The Trail, "blocking a bill that doesn't exist yet."[14]

DAILY, THEN DEEP DIVE, THEN DAILY AGAIN

Beyond the daily online battles to shed sunlight on the warrantless wiretapping efforts of the Bush administration, there were other strategies developed to provide long-form context to the fight.

Books have long served to certify political commentators as experts, giving them the gravitas to take their arguments out into the larger public sphere. In the networked media environment, they also serve as platforms for activism and continued commentary.

Inspired by high-profile progressive bestsellers such as George Lakoff's 2004 *Don't Think of an Elephant!*, progressive telephone company Working Assets decided to underwrite the effort to publish and promote Greenwald's *How Would a Patriot Act? Defending American Values from a President Run Amok.* Jennifer Nix, a longtime media producer and book editor, explained the process in a 2006 article titled "How to Create a Liberal Bestseller":

> On February 15, I asked Greenwald if he'd like to do a book. Working Assets stepped up to fund the project and launch Working Assets Publishing. By March 1, we had a contract and Greenwald sat down to write. There was a printer to find, a distributor to lure, an editorial team to assemble, and all of it managed by a quickly formed publishing division at the San Francisco headquarters of Working Assets. After some very long days, we delivered the book to the printer

> on April 24. The day before, I sent digital manuscripts to seven bloggers I'd been working with and asked them to post about the book, if they found it worthy. Within days *How Would a Patriot Act?* rose from obscurity to number one on Amazon largely because those initial blogs ignited a wildfire of mentions and purchase links throughout the blogosphere. The book stayed there for nearly four days. This sent a shock wave through progressive publishing circles and got stores around the country interested in making *Patriot* buys. The book's publication date was May 15 and since then has hit the *Washington Post* and *New York Times* bestseller list.[15]

The book, based on Greenwald's early Unclaimed Territory pieces, examined how the Bush administration used fear to radically expand its executive powers. Books by conservative commentators (such as Jerome Corsi; see Chapter 5) are often helped up the bestseller list by big purchases from conservative book clubs. Nix notes that *How Would a Patriot Act?*,

> rose to best-sellerdom primarily because of the pre-launch push from progressive blogs. Later came a front-page *San Francisco Chronicle* piece, some trade coverage and small mentions in the *New York Times* and the *New York Observer*, but this book has received very little mainstream coverage. No TV, a little radio—mostly Air America. Working Assets did send an e-mail blast about the book, and we got some help from a few organizations, like Drinking Liberally, American Constitution Society, Independent Press Association, and NDN/New Politics Institute. But the book has not received help from the big membership groups.

This is a success story and a tipping point for the blogosphere," she observed. "Greenwald went from first-time blogger to best-selling author in a little over six months on the strength of his ideas, which were formulated online, and the distribution power made possible by the Internet."

Simon Rosenberg, head of the New Democratic Network, told the *San Francisco Chronicle* that he hoped the book would be "the start of a liberal counterbalance to major conservative book clubs, whose combined membership of 100,000 regularly pushes books up the charts through presale orders."[16]

"That *Patriot* is coming out next week in a 15th century medium is a calculated decision," wrote *Chronicle* reporter Joe Garofoli. "Politically, said author Greenwald, it is easier to make a strong, cohesive argument in a book rather than in a three-paragraph burst on a blog. Plus, say marketers connected with the project, having a bound volume with your name on it makes it easier to build credibility with TV reporters and other 'mainstream media' types still suspicious of bloggers."[17]

Reviews of the book were scarce; its unorthodox launch initially earned it more ink than its content. But it did the trick. Greenwald was established as an expert on the administration's violations of civil liberties, and began to appear as a source in both mainstream and progressive outlets. His credibility in such arenas is underscored by the fact that he doesn't himself claim to be a progressive; rather, describes himself as an advocate for civil rights and the balance of powers described in the Constitution. This stance is the basis for the one-two punches he continues to deliver on his blog, allowing him to follow nearly in real time the themes he lays out in *How Would a Patriot Act?* and subsequent books.

Since then, progressives have organized to more formally develop support for book distribution by bloggers and advocacy groups. The Progressive Book Club, launched in June 2008, offers both breaking titles and community tools to connect readers, activists, and authors around issues. The club serves as a lens, focusing readers and funders on books designed to shift policy and build movements.

PILING ON THE PRESSURE

After Dodd's October 18 announcement, Greenwald, TPM and the bloggers kept the pressure on. On October 19, Senator Joe Biden (D-Del.)—also a presidential candidate—said he'd join Dodd's hold and proposed filibuster.[18] Feingold issued a statement promising to fight a bill offering immunity "vigorously with every tool at my disposal." Reid, however, was vacillating.[19] But then the *Wired* blog Threat Level broke the news that Senator Jay Rockefeller (D-W. Va.)—one of the strongest proponents of retroactive immunity for the telecom companies—had received substantial contributions in 2007 from AT&T and Verizon execs. As it turned out, AT&T was also one of the top twenty contributors to Harry Reid.[20]

A YouTube video of Dodd pledging to filibuster the bill if Reid refused to honor the hold stoked the flames further, spurring the bloggers and MoveOn to turn their attention to two other Democratic presidential candidates in the Senate: Hillary Clinton and Barack Obama.[21] TPM's Sargent reported on this new push, calling the Obama and Clinton offices for responses.[22] Clinton expressed her support of the filibuster in an October 23 press conference in Colorado, reported Sargent.[23] Obama issued a series of statements, each more definitive than the next, as the calls and coverage escalated. On October 24, campaign spokesman Bill Burton told TPM, "To be clear: Barack will support a filibuster of any bill that includes retroactive immunity for telecommunications companies."[24]

The proposed Senate bill granting immunity was effectively dead in the water, torpedoed by the joint actions of bloggers, reporters, and MoveOn members. "The most significant and encouraging aspect of all of this, by far, has been that all of this has happened solely because tens of thousands of people devoted to the rule of law and our basic Constitutional liberties have demanded it," wrote Greenwald in an October 24 post. "That has single-handedly catalyzed Dodd's leadership, compelled the other candidates to speak out against amnesty, and has forced attention to be paid to these issues. That progress—all achieved in barely a single week—is significant and should not be overlooked."[25]

BACK ON THE WARPATH

FISA cropped up again in mid-November, when the House passed H.R. 3773, known as the RESTORE Act (an unwieldy acronym standing for "Responsible Electronic Surveillance That Is Overseen, Reviewed, and Effective"). The act would reinstate court review of electronic surveillance of Americans' calls and e-mails, calling for individual warrants for wiretapping U.S. citizens.[26] Mixing it up with *Time* columnist Joe Klein, who dismissed the bill as "well beyond stupid,"[27] Greenwald minced no words:

> Yesterday—Saturday night on Thanksgiving weekend—Klein returned to the *Time* blog to write an extremely conditional, weaselly, self-justifying and partial "correction" to what he wrote in the print magazine. There's no indication whether any correction will appear in the print magazine, but the online version of Klein's article contains no such correction and still contains all of his grave misstatements.
>
> I don't want the focus here to be on Klein himself. It's beyond well-established what he is and what a slothful, easily manipulated and dishonest "reporter" he is. . . . What I want to do is examine Klein's conduct here to illustrate how so many Beltway reporters (though not all) function. This is not a matter of some obscure error involving details. Because of what Klein did, *Time Magazine* told its 4 million readers that the bill passed by the House Democrats "would give terrorists the same legal protections as Americans" and thus shows how Democrats still can't be trusted on national secu-

> rity. The whole column was built on complete, transparent falsehoods about the key provisions of that bill.[28]

Greenwald's crusade against Klein soon turned into an extended takedown of mainstream media for their faulty reporting on the war, which then escalated into a highly symbolic pissing match between old media and new.

Klein began backtracking, admitting, "I have neither the time nor legal background to figure out who's right."[29] As Hamsher and Greenwald dogged *Time* editors to find out who had approved the column, House Democrats began to get in on the act. Rep. Rush Holt (D-N.J.), one of the bill's authors, debunked Klein's column on the Huffington Post.[30] After issuing two separate corrections, *Time* finally asserted that "Republicans and Democrats interpret it differently," despite the fact that the bill never actually called for warrants for foreign surveillance suspects—Klein's original claim.

"*Time* has now concocted this fantasy where there is now some sort of raging dispute in Congress about whether the House Democrats' bill can be read to give the same rights to foreign terrorists as it does to U.S. citizens—a dispute which is simply non-existent in reality," raged Greenwald.[31]

Such disputes about mainstream reporting become flashpoints for partisan framing from both sides. As a result of the controversy, Rep. Peter Hoekstra (R-Mich.) revealed himself in the conservative *National Review* to be one of Klein's sources on the topic.[32]

"At the end of the day, we should be honest that this is not a legal debate, but a political one," wrote Hoekstra. "It highlights the fact that Democrats believe that lawyering-up foreign intelligence to guard against every imagined or potential civil-liberties concern is more important than ensuring that we have the full capability to conduct quick and effective surveillance of foreign al-Qaeda targets in foreign countries. I'll welcome that debate anytime."

As it turned out, he'd have plenty of chances to debate the point further. Skirmishes over FISA legislation continued in the House and Senate throughout the spring of 2008. On February 1, Keith Olbermann delivered one of his patented "Special Comments" on Bush's request for Congress to grant retroactive immunity to the telecoms during his State of the Union address—calling it a "textbook example of fascism" consisting of a compact between government and corporate interests.[33] Dodd cited Greenwald again in a marathon debate session on the Senate Floor on February 11.[34] On March 14, the House passed a new bill incorporating parts of both the RESTORE Act and the Senate's FISA Amendments Act of 2007. But a paucity of votes in the Senate held up the measure.

In early June, Republicans found themselves facing the looming expiration of orders put in place by the Protect America Act that had temporarily lifted FISA restrictions. In response, Senator Christopher S. Bond (R-Mo.) authored legislation that would amend FISA, omitting many of the privacy protections contained in earlier House bills. On June 9, a coalition of civil liberties organizations issued a joint statement in opposition to the bill. "Touted as a compromise to end an impasse between House and Senate versions of FISA legislation, the bill proposed by Senator Bond is far from a compromise," said the letter. "Neither Sen. Bond nor the administration has made a persuasive case that these sweeping new powers are needed or that existing authorities are inadequate to ensure the effectiveness of U.S. intelligence-gathering activities."[35]

For progressive bloggers, reporters, and activists, this was a call back to the barricades.

STRANGE BEDFELLOWS AND GETTING FISA RIGHT

Out of all of this jostling rose new networks and tactics. On June 17, Greenwald announced the formation of a broad alliance of bloggers, advocates, and organizations to take down members of Congress who supported telcom immunity and warrantless eavesdropping. Their first target was to be House majority leader Steny Hoyer (D-Md.). Hoyer was a leader in bipartisan meetings involving the House and Senate, reported *Roll Call*, to "hash out the remaining sticking points on legislation to update the 1979 Foreign Intelligence Surveillance Act."[36]

The progressive Web site Raw Story ran coverage of the new alliance—as well as a related effort—in a June 20 piece:

> The American Civil Liberties Union is teaming with supporters of former Republican presidential candidate Ron Paul and scores of liberal bloggers to pressure Congress on the surveillance law; the effort is calling itself Strange Bedfellows. . . . Parallel to the civil liberties' lobbying push is an effort being spearheaded by the Blue America PAC that aims to raise $350,000 to campaign against lawmakers who support giving immunity to the telecommunications companies, including moderate and conservative Democrats. Markos Moulitsas, founder of DailyKos, laid bare the challenge Thursday: "When we started this 'netroots' thing, we worked to get 'more and better Democrats' elected. At first, we focused on the 'more' part. This year, we're focusing a bit more on the 'better' part. And in 2010, we'll have enough Democrats in the House to exclusively focus on the 'better' part.
>
> "That means primary challenges. And as we decide who to take on, let it be known that this FISA vote will loom large."[37]

June 19 was a productive day for the Strange Bedfellows. In concert with the campaign the Blue America PAC had managed to raise $200,000. Activists were calling Obama's campaign to demand an intervention on the so-called compromise bill. The

ACLU's Caroline Fredrickson denounced the bill as allowing "mass and untargeted surveillance of Americans' communications," and Feingold dismissed it as not a compromise but a "capitulation." On June 20, the Blue America PAC teamed up with Color of Change—a mobilizing group similar to MoveOn that focuses on organizing African Americans—to place an ad in the *Washington Post* denouncing Hoyer for his FISA stance.[38] The ad drew comparisons between warrantless wiretapping and the 1960s surveillance of prominent civil rights leaders, conjuring up both powerful associations and the specter of racism.

But by the 21st, the political tides had shifted. Obama announced his support of the bill, dashing hopes that he would take part in the filibuster promised the previous October.

This decision by the presidential hopeful struck many as political jockeying, an effort by Obama to appear tough on terrorists and toe a bipartisan line. In the eyes of progressive bloggers and journalists, however, this was no centrist decision. In a post on the 24th, Greenwald wrote:

> I was just on a conference call with Obama foreign policy advisor Dennis McDonough. The Huffington Post's Scott Bellows asked about Obama's abandonment of his rhetoric vowing to defend the Constitution in order to support this bill, and McDonough adopted the Hoyer line, claiming that this bill has all sorts of great oversight protections including the requirement that the Inspector General submit a report on Bush's spying program. That's what now passes for oversight in our Government—the Executive branch investigates itself when it comes to allegations of criminality. Whatever else is true, there's just no getting around the fact that Obama—when seeking the nomination—vowed to support a filibuster of any bill that contains telecom immunity, and his failure to do that here will be a patent breach of that commitment. There's still time for him to adhere to that promise.[39]

Meanwhile, a fresh network of citizen activists was self-organizing, using the Obama campaign's own social network, MyBarackObama.com, as a platform. On July 3, the *Washington Post*'s Jose Antonio Vargas reported that the Get FISA Right group had already grown to sixteen thousand members—the largest group on the site.[40]

Obama's response to this development was diplomatic but firm. "Now, I understand why some of you feel differently about the current bill, and I'm happy to take my lumps on this site and elsewhere. For the truth is that your organizing, your activism and your passion is an important reason why this bill is better than previous versions," he wrote. "I cannot promise to agree with you on every issue. But I do promise to listen to your concerns, take them seriously, and seek to earn your ongoing support to change the country . . . Democracy cannot exist without strong differences. And going forward, some of you may decide that my FISA position is a deal breaker. That's OK. But I think it is worth pointing out that our agreement on the vast majority of issues that matter outweighs the differences we may have."[41]

The emergence of the Get FISA Right group marked a new phase in the communication between politicians and pressure groups made up of thousands of individuals. While such organizing built upon the campaigns that bloggers had built, it also stole some of their thunder as high-profile intermediaries. Social networks such as Facebook and MySpace had already begun to challenge the primacy of Web sites and blogs as first-resort spots for breaking news, and the evolution of targeted social networks created yet more fragmentation.

On his aptly named blog, Liminal States, Jon Pincus, a lead organizer of the Get FISA Right effort, described the early weeks of the campaign:

> Get FISA Right's start as a group of Senator Obama's supporters using my.barackobama.com (myBO) to put pressure

> on him, and then evolving to a "50-state strategy", really highlights the power of social network-based movements. We quickly became the largest group on myBO, and then Obama replied to our open letter giving more details about his position on the Foreign Intelligence Surveillance Act (FISA) amendment than he had discussed with the press. Even though he didn't change his position, sometimes all you can say is "w00t w00t!"
>
> At that point, we cracked the mainstream media (MSM) in a big way: The NY Times! Time! Meet the Press! And I did my part too: on Radio Nation's Air America, mentions in a bunch of articles including the Washington Post and Wired, a brief snippet on CNN . . . fifteen seconds of fame :-)
>
> While the July 9 vote on FISA was incredibly disappointing, it was also marked continued progress for the pro–civil liberties forces—all the more impressive because in early July, I had heard from Washington insiders that they were concerned that as few as 14 Senators might vote against the legislation, and it turned out to be 28. To be sure, Get FISA Right (GFR) was only one part of a larger effort, but we certainly contributed a new hook to the story, brought in a lot of new people, and were able to get significant mainstream media (MSM) coverage.[42]

Pincus credits the tech/politics blogs as well as progressive bloggers and media outlets for initially drawing attention to GFR. But he goes on to identify a number of sticking points for self-organizing networks of activists seeking to work with the progressive blogosphere. First off, there's bloggers' skepticism about the social network activists. "It's kind of amusing to hear bloggers use the same kinds of dismissive comments about social network sites that people were making about them a few years ago, but from an activism perspective it's very disappointing,"[43] writes Pincus. He also notes large gaps between the political blogosphere and feminist, antiracist, and LGBTQ blogs—a common complaint that we'll address more directly in Chapter 9. Both issues have to do with the ever-increasing democratization of communications platforms.

Carlo Scannella, a graduate student at the New School, also wrote about his experience working on GFR. He quotes Clay Shirky, the author of *Here Comes Everybody: The Power of Organizing without Organizations*: "Communications tools don't get socially interesting until they get technologically boring."

"By this, he means that it's not until technologies become ubiquitous and commonplace and, indeed, boring, do they enable profound social changes," writes Scannella.

> For the Get FISA Right group, this meant two things. First, the technologies themselves had to be free, readily available, and easy to use. Tools like Wetpaint and Google Groups 'pages,' and sites like Facebook meant there were platforms around which we could collaborate. But beyond the tools themselves, for this group, collaborating online was 'boring.' Many of the group members were already well-versed in blogs and wikis, and were able to quickly acclimate to the unique social norms and cohesiveness required to be productive online.

What's more, Scannella noted, while bloggers have fixed communities, "netroots" campaigns organized across multiple social networks are effectively rootless.

> The Get FISA Right group has no home. We're distributed; nomadic. We're a Google group and a chat room and a wiki that is constantly changing. We're a collection of email

> messages in the ether. Perhaps that will change. Since our work started, we've created an Internet domain. We have a logo. Perhaps one day, there will be some roots.[44]

But by early 2009, GFR members had already migrated to even more platforms: a blog, Twitter, new sites such as Change .gov, and government transparency sites such as Ask the President and Ask Your Lawmaker.[45] Did this count as progressive media-making? Organizing? Both—or neither? Hard to say. One thing was clear, though: increasingly "boring" social media tools were making it more and more interesting for progressives to take their issues to the hill.

MAKING A HOME ON THE HILL

While bloggers, activists, and progressive journalists can make their mark on policy making through the kinds of concerted organizing described above, there's another way for progressive outlets to impact politics: to report from inside the Beltway itself.

Established in 1990, the *American Prospect* (TAP) was founded by political commentators and academics Robert Kuttner, Robert Reich, and Paul Starr "as an authoritative magazine of liberal ideas, committed to a just society, an enriched democracy, and effective liberal politics."[46]

The magazine, which publishes ten times a year and maintains a daily Web site, offers readers around the country a deep dive into policy debates by combining quality reporting with policy analysis that adds a human dimension to political and social issues. *TAP* is also known for its Writing Fellowships Program, which fosters young journalistic talents with a two-year tenure at the outlet. Young talent does seem to regularly flow through this publication, from "liberal darling"[47] Ezra Klein (who moved to the *Washington Post* in May 2009) to Ann Friedman, *TAP*'s deputy editor and one of the editors of Feministing.com (more on Feministing in Chapter 9).

Mark Schmitt, who joined *TAP* in mid-2007 as executive editor, believes that to be more effective on the Hill as a journalism organization, you cannot focus on advocating for particular issues or pushing Congress to the left, because you will "suffer as a news outlet and web site. If you view the Hill as what you are about, you are always caught up in the definition of what's defined as possible on the Hill at that moment," he says.

Schmitt contends that the key for *TAP* is to focus more on the substance of policy and ideas that aren't necessarily on the radar at the moment. "If we're hitting the mark, we're balancing being both aspirational and looking at possibilities of what's bigger on the agenda right now—as well as being realistic," he says. One of the key tools for *TAP* is the "special packages" that are produced several times per year in the magazine, which allow the reporting to delve even more deeply into issues. "We can combine journalism and put forth a rich set of ideas that have some heft and reality to them," Schmitt explains.

But whether it's their stand-alone reporting or special packages, Schmitt has a different perspective on building community online than others do. As a journalistic organization, Schmitt believes *TAP*'s strength lies in a forum approach—not generated by users, but compiled and edited by staff and experts with key areas of knowledge around a particular topic.

As we explore in the next chapter, bringing the progressive community together through this and other strategies can have significant consequences for the political future of the country.

8
ASSEMBLE THE PROGRESSIVE CHOIR

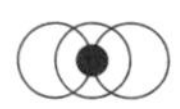

The trial was in full swing. The defendant: Vice President Dick Cheney's top aide, I. Lewis "Scooter" Libby Jr. The witnesses: Judith Miller of the *New York Times*, Matt Cooper of *Newsweek*, and Tim Russert, host of *Meet the Press*, among others.

As 2007 began, Libby was facing five counts, including perjury, for his role in leaking the identity of CIA agent Valerie Plame Wilson to conservative pundit Robert Novak, who revealed the agent's name in a July 2003 *Chicago Sun-Times* column. But while Libby was the only person formally on trial, the establishment media was also under public indictment for its role in the resulting quagmire.

Throughout U.S. Attorney Patrick Fitzgerald's investigation into the leak, it became clear that the establishment journalists' many connections to Washington political elites had muddled their reporting decisions. Their reluctance to accurately report on conservative think tanks' and commentators' spin jobs in the lead-up to the Iraq war—much less the role of former Vice President Cheney's office in the leak—was under the microscope. As Michael Massing, the author of *Now They Tell Us: The American Press and Iraq*, wrote in the *New York Review of Books*:

> The Plame leak case has provided further insight into the relation between the journalistic and political establishments. It's now clear that Lewis Libby was an important figure in the White House and a key architect of the administration's push for war in Iraq. Many journalists seem to have

> spoken with him regularly, and to have been fully aware of his power, yet virtually none bothered to inform the public about him, much less scrutinize his actions on behalf of the vice-president. A search of major newspapers in the fifteen months before the war turned up exactly one substantial article about Libby—a breezy piece by Elisabeth Bumiller in the *New York Times* about his novel *The Apprentice*.[1]

Simultaneously forced to cover the trial, explain their role to the public, and testify on the stand, mainstream reporters were also looking askance at a group of six unlikely individuals who attended the trial every day. Sharing two press passes, they rotated to enter the trial each morning, transcribing the proceedings almost word for word. Throughout the trial, these unconventional observers provided daily, sometimes hourly, analysis of the proceedings and offered critiques of establishment media coverage.

"All day long during the trial, one Firedoglake blogger is on duty to beam to the Web from the courthouse media room a rough, real-time transcript of the testimony," noted a February 15, 2007, article from the *New York Times*. "With no audio or video feed permitted, the FireDogLake 'live blog' has offered the fullest, fastest public report available. Many mainstream journalists use it to check on the trial."[2]

After the trial was over, Firedoglake (FDL) blogger "Scarecrow" covered a panel at the annual Yearly Kos conference, where two other FDL bloggers—Christy Hardin-Smith and Marcy Wheeler—recounted their experiences. "As Marcy noted today, the bloggers knew what none in the MSM every [*sic*] admitted, that the Libby trial was just as much about the media's complicity and its seduction by the favors of privileged access as [the] lies and obstruction of Scooter Libby and Dick Cheney," Scarecrow wrote. "And when the verdict came down, it was not just Libby who was found guilty, but some of the best known media personalities as well."[3]

Covering the Libby trial was the high point of what had been a whirlwind few years for the FDL crew—which included becoming one of the most popular blogs in the country. The attention they received during the trial was one of the first times mainstream reporters had acknowledged bloggers for their prowess as journalists. But what really set FDL apart was the influence that the site had built with its active and engaged community. The site had developed the power to move their users to rally around campaigns that included exposing mainstream media failures and raising hundreds of thousands of dollars for progressive candidates.

FDL's ability to merge journalism with action set up a new power dynamic for progressive media organizations—not just preaching to a passionate choir, but moving them directly to action.

STRATEGIC OPPORTUNITIES

The left is often derided for "preaching to the choir." Detractors argue that communicating with the already converted does little to bring in new audiences and merely reinforces accepted beliefs. Others believe that "preaching to the choir" limits debate and access to alternative viewpoints.

In a 2007 *Chronicle of Higher Education* article, Cass Sunstein, a University of Chicago law professor, wrote about the dangers of people seeking viewpoints that match their own:

> As a result of the Internet, we live increasingly in an era of enclaves and niches—much of it voluntary, much of it produced by those who think they know, and often do know, what we're likely to like. This raises some obvious questions. If people are sorted into enclaves and niches, what will happen to their views? What are the eventual effects on democracy? . . . A key consequence of this kind of self-sorting is what we might call enclave extremism. When people end up

> in enclaves of like-minded people, they usually move toward a more extreme point in the direction to which the group's members were originally inclined.[4]

But others who operate within the politicized media space believe that reaching out and engaging the like-minded has an inherent and long-ignored value. Wrote blogger Chris Bowers earlier in 2007:

> By preaching to our choir, and organizing that choir, the progressive blogosphere and netroots have grown to wield a large amount of influence within the progressive political ecosystem simply by harnessing progressive energy that had lain dormant and ignored for so long. Just as importantly, harnessing this energy has also greatly enhanced the capability of the progressive political ecosystem as a whole, by making better use of all the available resources in that ecosystem. As we have seen over the past few years, all that new money, media influence, activism, strategy, infrastructure and ideas generated in this new constituency have not just played a major role within the progressive political ecosystem, but within the broader American political ecosystem as well. If the progressive netroots had been so myopic to only and ever target the "swing," that energy would probably still be untapped, and progressives would be at the same disastrous level of infrastructure disadvantage to conservative that we were during the 1990's and the early parts of this decade."[5]

As noted in previous chapters, the right had successfully built its noise machine precisely by creating ideological vehicles to amass, inform and activate conservative audiences. From think tanks such as the Heritage Foundation, to magazines such as the *Weekly Standard*, talking heads such as Ann Coulter, and shock jocks such as Rush Limbaugh, conservatives not only constructed their own media equivalent of a megachurch but assembled a choir loud enough to be heard across the entire media landscape, significantly influencing policy debates and elections.

But "preaching" is actually a false description of what many progressive projects do. While they may exhort audiences via editorials and essays, those progressive outlets devoted explicitly to journalism spend much more time investigating, reporting, and informing their audiences about political and social debates, trends, and events. And for the more activist media outlets—most notably the bloggers—the term "preaching" falls flat, as it assumes one-way communication without any conversation or collective reaction.

As Bowers notes, it is the *assembling* and activating of the choir that is the critical strategy. Just as churches, temples, or mosques serve as hubs for those seeking to examine and fortify their beliefs, a number of media outlets have evolved into central meeting places for those looking to join, debate, and strengthen political movements.

Sites such as FDL resemble the movement publications of previous generations, springing up around a particular political moment and working explicitly to attract and organize like-minded users. In *People's Movements, People's Press: The Journalism of Social Justice Movements*, Bob Ostertag writes about the pivotal role that newspapers and magazines served in U.S. political movements of the last two centuries, including abolition, women's suffrage, gay and lesbian liberation, anti–Vietnam War activism, and environmentalism:

> People in positions of institutional power, whether generals, politicians, bankers, and even journalists, exercise some degree of social power during the course of their everyday professional lives. For everyone else, if we seek to have a voice in shaping our society beyond our immediate social circle, we

have to step outside our daily existence into roles to which we are not accustomed and for which we have little or no institutional support. We have to band together to maximize our very limited time and resources. Before we can do any of that, we have to find each other—identify others with the same interests who are also willing to step outside their daily lives to pursue our long-shot objectives. We have to see who's good at what, who else is doing what, who might rise to the occasion if given half a chance. We have to make plans, formulate strategies, set priorities. We have to agitate, educate, mobilize, confront and more. In short, we have to constitute ourselves as a political subject, a constituency, a *social movement*. And if we had done this sometime between 1830 and 2000, we would have made a newspaper. In most cases, it would have been the first thing we did.[6]

From 2000 to 2008, the first thing that many activists and journalists did to join and define the progressive movement was to start a blog. But while many blogs offer a relatively narrow framework for participating in politics, other progressive media projects are more ecumenical. Ostertag distinguishes such focused outlets from those that "contributed to many movements yet were not rooted in any particular one," such as *Mother Jones*, *I. F. Stone's Weekly*, and "the granddaddy of them all," *The Nation*, published since 1865.

In his 2005 book *A Matter of Opinion*, Victor Navasky, former editor and publisher of *The Nation*, provides a lively account of the magazine's role in national and global politics:

> I always get a big laugh when people dismiss *The Nation* (or any journal of opinion) by saying that it "preaches to the choir" or is dogmatic or ideological or follows a party line. Barely a week has gone by in my years at *The Nation* when I have not had to answer a letter, a phone call, or, in more

> recent years, e-mail from an unharmonious dissident member of the so-called choir. And rather than march in lockstep, our contributors and staffers have disagreed, argued, feuded and debated, among themselves and in our pages, on matters of principle, practicality, politics, policy and morality.[7]

Indeed, Navasky offers a dizzying catalog of the range of positions and issues that have been battled out on the pages (and, later, the Web pages) of *The Nation*, placing the current progressive surge in proper historical context. Throughout, however, he asserts the value of providing a weekly space to "question the conventional wisdom, to be suspicious of all orthodoxies, to provide a home for dissent and dissenters, and, to be corny about it, to hold forth a vision of a better world."[8]

As Navasky—who writes that the main role for *The Nation* has been to "serve as a forum for the debate between the radicals and the liberals"[9]—suggests, the progressive community is made of many factions of choirs. Sometimes these factions will join together around a certain political moment, event, or policy. But very rarely are they all in concert (with the monumental exception of their dislike for the former Bush administration), and more often than not, such alliances can quickly disintegrate.

A major question—one we tackle in more detail in the next chapter—is: who gets to define the choir? Age, gender, race, sexual preference, personal style, cultural preferences, and ideology all play into the creation and success of particular political outlets.

In the networked media environment, the trick is to learn how to regularly sync or "assemble" these diverse choirs for maximum engagement and action. As we note in the chapter "Build a Network-Powered Media," online platforms have offered progressives powerful tools to attract and organize their users, hold those in power accountable, and raise up those who share similar values and ideals. The result has been the rise of a dynamic infrastructure that has shored up the left's ability to affect the political process.

While early blogs showcased the insights, media criticism, reporting, and, yes, rants of individuals, they soon turned into political communities, offering a space for their users to help develop and debate political and social justice strategies. Discussion platforms—such as forums for community comments and diaries that allowed users themselves to blog—hastened the growth of the progressive choir, as did technologies that allowed bloggers to link to, feature, and argue with one another.

The key element for running such sites is regular conversations with users. The most successful "assemblers" don't just post a story or analysis and then lurk in the background and read comments and reactions. They dive back into the community debate, expand their argument, discuss users' reactions, and even sometimes reframe their own outlook based on community feedback. This is an inclusive process: Media producers may have the higher profile, but their transparency keeps them accountable to their community. Such two-way communication between the outlet and its community also allows for an environment of trust to develop. Bloggers and editors know that their site's ongoing influence is dependent on the community's knowledge that the media producer is credible and accessible.

As the community grows, the outlet gains more power to validate ideological points of view in the larger public debate. This is key in moments when the outlet works to move its community to action via online and offline protests, such as boycotts, donations, or letters of support. This is where true impact is revealed—driving tens of thousands to a certain action can result in media coverage and larger public recognition of an issue or policy. Combining "crowd-swarming" and media coverage can result in the ultimate goal: a reaction, a capitulation, or an agreement from the target of ire, whether it is a government official, a corporation, or even another journalist.

In this chapter we explore two different models of assembling the progressive choir. While Firedoglake demonstrates an innovative, high-impact activist approach, AlterNet, an online news source that republishes content for a wide range of progressive outlets, serves as sort of choir of choirs, amplifying and expanding the sector.

HOW FIREDOGLAKE BECAME ONE OF THE LEFT'S BEST "ASSEMBLERS"

Firedoglake has broken ground as a Web-native hybrid: a media outlet and an organizer of the left. Founded in 2004 by Jane Hamsher, a former movie producer of such films as *Natural Born Killers* and *Apt Pupil*, FireDogLake was a spin-off from Hamsher's involvement in the community on Daily Kos, where she would frequently comment.

Hamsher says she was initially drawn to the political blogosphere during the Whitewater trial, when she says she found herself wanting to throw things daily at the television. Throughout her interactions on Daily Kos, she found herself drawn to the possibilities of what an online-networked group of people could accomplish.

"What interested me was Ralph Reed," Hamsher says, referring to how Reed had been able to organize the churches in the 1980s. "I was interested in seeing this self-existing architecture of the churches that he could just network together. . . . He was the one who took it and used it to get presidents elected." She notes that until the blogosphere, "there was no natural place for me to network with people who felt like I did. So suddenly I saw this and thought, 'wow.' So it's been a constant process over the last four years of exploring different ways to do that, but with the ultimate goal of networking progressives together in order to have an effect on the culture, the country, the world . . . an effect beyond the numbers."

Hamsher's strategy for building an effective network of progressives was to offer users a place where they could talk and feel part of something larger. She wanted to create an environment that addressed their needs, cared what they thought, and, last but not least, responded to their criticisms.

Hamsher and her fellow FDL bloggers— including "redhead" (Hardin-Smith), "emptywheel" (Wheeler), "Siun" (Christina Siun O'Connell), and those who like to be known by their aliases only, such as "Pachacutec" and "T-Bogg"—have turned this engaged space into a media juggernaut and a spot for one-off and ongoing organizing.

For FDL, 2006 was a seminal year. One initial organizing or "assembling" attempt included the Roots Project, timed to influence congressional hearings on the National Security Administration's warrantless wiretapping efforts. FDL partnered with blogger Glenn Greenwald and John Amato of the video blog Crooks and Liars to recruit small groups of local activists. They sought out constituents of senators who might wield swing votes to write letters to the editors of their local newspapers. The hope was that an outcry in local outlets might pressure the senators "to vote for real oversight in the face of illegal executive overreach." [10]

The Roots Project provided the context for local and statewide groups of activists to self-organize on a range of issues. In general, those issues were dictated by the local groups, but the groups could also connect with each other to more fully take on national issues. The project provided tools for individuals within the groups to find, meet, and contact one another, and to organize and advertise events, as well as to contact media outlets and their congressional representatives. Much of this seems rudimentary now, but back then, it was a revelation for a group of blogs to come together and provide the space for users to self-organize and take action.

The year 2006 was also a big watershed in terms of bloggers organizing users around midterm electoral politics. With Crooks and Liars and the blog Down with Tyranny run by Howie Klein (Hamsher knew Klein as a DJ in San Francisco many years before), FDL formed the Blue America PAC, designed to raise money for progressive congressional candidates. Hosted on the ActBlue .com site, an online clearinghouse for Democratic campaign fund-raising, Blue America raised just over $544,000 for congressional candidates from 6,053 supporters in 2006 and another $448,000 from 5,362 supporters in 2008.[11]

What motivated these individuals to donate? Along with the new ease of making online donations and learning about candidates (even candidates across the country), Hamsher claims that the site's basic ideology was the impetus.

"I realized our audience was very active and had a very strong sense of social justice and right and wrong—and that continues to characterize FDL to this day. A lot of other blogs during the election decided that they were wholesaling to one candidate over the other. We never really got into that—the politics of personality. I think that we've always stayed principle-focused," says Hamsher.

FDL would bring the candidates and potential donors together in virtual kaffeeklatsches. Candidates looking for supporters would join the FDL community for live Q&A chats where they would answer users' questions about policies, ideology, and what they would do once elected. This tactic removed traditional barriers and allowed candidates to more easily reach out to supporters across the country. Without this infrastructure, many of the FDL users would never have had the opportunity to openly and directly converse with the candidates. This direct communication is an integral part of Blue America's candidate fund-raising strategy.

In addition to fund-raising, FDL and a cohort of netroots allies decided to put their full attention, energy, and muscle behind overthrowing congressional incumbents who they believed had betrayed the progressive value system. Hamsher and Matt Stoller (then at the blog MyDD) became involved in millionaire businessman Ned Lamont's campaign to unseat Connecticut senator Joe Lieberman for the 2006 election. When Lamont announced his Senate candidacy against Lieberman, many thought it was beyond a long shot. But Lamont surprised observers as the national progressive blogosphere closed ranks behind his antiwar campaign.

Stoller and Hamsher traveled and lived in the state to cover the fierce primary election and encouraged their users to donate money and energy. Hamsher also encouraged the FDL community to travel to Connecticut and volunteer time to the campaign. The community responded—and volunteers from as far away as California traveled east to help with a last-minute primary push. Lamont drew upon the combined forces of the national progressive blogosphere, a set of ever-growing and more powerful local and state blogs, and good old-fashioned campaigning and turnout tactics. He stunned many when he beat Lieberman in the primary.

National and local progressive bloggers were triumphant with the victory. But Lieberman drew from his deep war chest and ran in the general election as an independent. By courting Republicans, he ended up winning, 50–40 percent.[12]

Despite the loss, the powerful role of the blogosphere was now getting attention. "Lamont, a millionaire with little political experience, catapulted from anonymity to become a front-running Senate candidate with the help of a new political phenomenon: bloggers," wrote Michael M. Grynbaum for the *Boston Globe*, on the day of the primary. "Political analysts say that the network of Internet commentators—some from as far away as California—channeled voter anger against veteran incumbent Senator Joseph I. Lieberman and his support for the Iraq war into a huge boost for Lamont, drawing national attention to the race. Lamont's strong challenge underscores the blogosphere's emergence as a new political power base, observers say."[13]

The campaign's initial success and the resulting press coverage were both validations and shocks for the FDL crew. "We just weren't ready for prime time. We'd been toiling [on] the edges, not thinking we were having any impact, but because it was the right thing to do . . . and all of a sudden we get shoved out into the mainstream. It was a real adjustment," says Hamsher. "[FDL blogger] Pachacutec compared the blog at the time to kids in the back of the room screaming, being the bad kids and throwing spitballs because nobody was paying any attention to us and that's how we [got] attention. And then all of a sudden, as our influence started to increase, we had to write in such a way that people took us seriously, but not lose the authentic personal voice that made people trust us and want to come and read us in the first place."

And then came the Libby trial. Before the trial even began, FDL put out a call across multiple blogs in September 2006, hoping to raise $65,000 to help publish *Anatomy of Deceit: How the Bush Administration Used the Media to Sell the Iraq War and Out a Spy* by Marcy Wheeler.

Wheeler had been tirelessly reporting and blogging at both FDL and Daily Kos about the complicity of the mainstream press in the outing of Plame. Hamsher and Markos Moulitsas commissioned Wheeler to turn her blogging and analysis into a book for their newly founded co-venture, Vaster Media. They wanted the book out in time for the start of the Libby trial, only months away. The call for funds raised $29,000.

Firedoglake's coverage of the Libby trial fueled the site's popularity and growth. By 2007, FDL had a team of almost twenty part-time bloggers in addition to Hamsher and Smith.[14] By 2008, it had become known as one of the top progressive blogs in the country. Hamsher claims that in October 2008, they had approximately 4.5 million page views.

One of Hamsher's proudest moments of 2008 came when FDL organized their audience to respond to a story by AP reporter Nedra Pickler, who reported on how Republican operatives were raising questions about Senator Barack Obama's patriotism. Wrote Eric Boehlert in his "Media Matters" column:

> What prompted the organized outpouring of angst last week against the AP was when the website Firedoglake took ac-

> tion, embraced a new organizing tool, tapped into a wellspring of enthusiasm for Obama, and pointed angry readers not in the direction of the AP itself, but toward their local newspaper clients. . . . The results, according to FDL, as of March 3: 14,252 letters sent to 649 different newspapers located in all 50 states, and from 1,735 ZIP codes. That included more than 1,500 letters to the *New York Times*, 1,400 to both *USA Today* and the *Washington Post*—not to mention 52 to the *Denver Post* and 21 to the *Florida Times-Union*.[15]

This was a creative jujitsu move, turning the power of mainstream media against itself. FDL's choir was singing, loud and proud enough for even the biggest outlets to hear them.

There are many examples like this—too many to count. With its weekly book salons, the site has become a hub and amplifier for the larger progressive community. FDL bloggers interact with community members via multiple daily posts, including political commentary, news roundups, and original reporting. Through its community blog, the Oxdown Gazette, and stepped-up field organizing, FDL provides regular opportunities for engagement and self-organizing. In the process, the site has established itself as one of the leading progressive outlets and assemblers of the decade.

A CHOIR OF CHOIRS

Part of what makes FDL work is its personal feel and targeted coverage. In contrast, AlterNet's executive editor, Don Hazen, describes his long-standing progressive portal as "the opposite of niche."

The site seeks to expand the audience for progressive news and cultural reporting—as its "About" page notes, "Many of AlterNet's readers come from search engines (like Google) and news aggregator sites (such as Digg or Reddit), a testament to the fact that AlterNet reaches beyond the typical 'choir' of progressive readers."[16] Once there, users encounter an ever-changing assortment of articles, blogs, video, live audio streams, book excerpts, and more. AlterNet produces some original coverage, but mostly it aggregates content from more than two hundred independent media outlets and blogs on a daily basis.

Hazen says he compares the selection process for each day's above-the-fold stories to creating a musical remix. "Remixing content is an art in and of itself—you want polemic, investigative reporting, sex, drugs, and rock and roll." He notes that he and other editors spend a lot of time crafting headlines that will attract clicks, noting that the goal of the site has always been to "get as much good content to as many eyeballs as possible." Controversial political moments create waves of new users—the announcement of Alaska governor Sarah Palin as Senator John McCain's running mate was a boon to the site, which lured anxious readers with provocative articles such as "Mad Dog Palin," "8 More Shocking Revelations About Sarah Palin" (number 5: "Crazy Reverend, Crazy Church"), and "The 11 Dumbest Things Sarah Palin Has Said So Far."

All of those teasers paid off. In 2008, AlterNet attracted an average of two million visits per month. Hazen credits their traffic numbers in part to AlterNet's longtime online presence. The project has its roots in print; founded in 1985 as the Institute for Alternative Journalism, it began as a wire service for alternative newsweeklies, packaging syndicated content from independent magazines for reprinting in local outlets. Hazen came on in 1991 on the heels of an idea to create a *Parade*-style insert for the alt weeklies, but soon found what "seemed like a brilliant idea at the time" to be a nonstarter. "Nobody thought about how difficult it would be to get people to collaborate," he says. Graced with a surplus of independent content, AlterNet's board members recognized the Internet as a natural platform for distribution. "We realized that we could become our own publisher," says Hazen, who changed the organization's name to the Independent Media Institute. AlterNet was launched in 1998.

AlterNet negotiates with magazines and blogs for permission to offer their articles online, with mixed success. Some outlets opt to retain control of the distribution of their own content online, while others see AlterNet's selection of their pieces as an "imprimatur of status." Today, Hazen sees the site's leading competitors as *Salon*, which produces much of its own content, and the Huffington Post, which relies heavily on links and aggregation. He distinguishes the site from progressive blogs such as Daily Kos, many of which have a narrow focus on gaining electoral wins.

Hazen describes the site's model as "strategic journalism"—reporting tethered to advocacy. Sometimes AlterNet staffers will team up with advocacy groups, not just to report on related issues but to craft ads that drive AlterNet readers to the organizations. "I haven't figured out the balance between activism and journalism," says Hazen, "and I don't know if anyone ever will."

Hazen says the site is still closer to an old-media, broadcast model than a diary-driven, user-generated blog. "Our main goal is to get the best stuff out to as many people as possible and have them do with it what they will."

AlterNet helps to support the expansion of the progressive media sector in other ways. It serves as a hub and amplifier for networked campaigns, working closely with producer-activists such as Robert Greenwald. Hazen himself regularly writes about the prospects and pitfalls of progressive media. In spring 2008 the site launched its own imprint, AlterNet Books, which published Rory O'Connor's *Shock Jocks: Hate Speech and Talk Radio.*[17] The book includes an analysis of how progressive radio personalities are beginning to counter conservative dominance on the dial.

Over the years, AlterNet has made a conscious effort to diversify its content, at times creating a self-imposed guideline for editors selecting the day's news so as to incorporate female writers and writers of color. But their challenge in doing so reflects a discrepancy in the progressive media choir itself.

Both legacy outlets and the progressive blogosphere are dominated by white, male, middle-class writers, editors, directors, producers, and pundits. In the next chapter, we take a look at a few progressive projects that serve audiences beyond the "pale, stale, and male."

9
MOVE BEYOND PALE, MALE, AND STALE

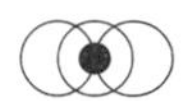

On September 20, 2007, tens of thousands of people descended on the town of Jena, Louisiana, to protest the incarceration of six black teenagers who had been charged with the attempted murder of a white student. The events leading up to the charges had all the makings of a story from the Deep South fifty years ago: nooses hanging from trees and black students harassed, assaulted, and then jailed.

The story of these high school students, known as the "Jena Six," encapsulated the simmering, but often ignored, issues of racism that continue to this day. The response to the exaggerated charges levied against them was the largest civil rights protest the country had seen in years.

But what had moved thousands of individuals from fury to action? Sure, the old-school civil rights organizations and activists, such as the NAACP, RainbowPUSH, and Al Sharpton, started crying foul in the lead-up to the protest. But they joined the ranks of protestors after the real organizing had been accomplished by an emergent group of networked individuals and organizations.

Howard Witt, a reporter for the *Chicago Tribune*, was the first establishment reporter tracking this case and the subsequent organizing. His article "Blogs Help Drive Jena Protest" threaded together the story of how this new coalition emerged.

> This will be a civil rights protest literally conjured out of the ether of cyberspace, of a type that has never happened before

> in America—a collective national mass action grown from a grassroots word-of-mouth movement spread via Internet blogs, e-mails, message boards and talk radio.
>
> Jackson, Sharpton and other big-name civil rights figures, far from leading this movement, have had to scramble to catch up. So, too, has the national media, which has only recently noticed a story that has been agitating many black Americans for months.
>
> As formidable as it is amorphous, this new African-American blogosphere, which scarcely even existed a year ago, now comprises hundreds of interlinked blogs and tens of the thousands of followers who within a matter of a few weeks collected 220,000 petition signatures—and more than $130,000 in donations for legal fees—in support of six black Jena teenagers who are being prosecuted on felony battery charges for beating a white student.[1]

The black blogosphere didn't emerge overnight; rather, its creation was a steady process in the making. Many of the individual black bloggers had emerged in reaction to different events, including the fatal shooting of Sean Bell by police officers in Queens, the racist remarks by radio shock jock Don Imus (we won't repeat them here), and the incarceration of Shaquanda Cotton (more on that below).

The 2008 presidential election also played a role in the development of the political arm of the black blogosphere. James Rucker, former software developer and MoveOn staffer, founded Color of Change in late 2005 shortly after Hurricane Katrina to "empower our members—Black Americans and our allies—to make government more responsive to the concerns of Black Americans and to bring about positive political and social change for everyone."[2] In 2007, the organization launched a high-profile campaign with Brave New Films and its Fox Attacks campaign, MoveOn, and blogs such as MyDD and Daily Kos to force the Nevada Democratic Party to cancel a presidential debate sponsored by the Congressional Black Caucus because it was scheduled for broadcast on Fox News. Multiplatform media production, large-scale organizing, and local on-the-ground action made for a winning progressive media formula, defeating the efforts of an influential national conservative media outlet.

Rucker noted the import of the broad coalition around the cancellation of the debate and specifically the reach of Color of Change and the black blogosphere. The campaign demonstrated to black elected officials that an emerging powerful online group could call them out when they took actions that harmed their core constituents. Chris Rabb, founder of the blog Afro-Netizen, cut to the chase in an early April post:

> Why is the [Congressional] Black Caucus [CBC] condoning the anti-Black and, specifically, anti-Obama onslaught waged by the Fox New[s] Channel, and remaining silent on the CBC Institute's recent announcement to collaborate with Fox to air two presidential debates? . . . Do these [CBC] folks know what the "netroots" is? Do they think it's just made up of young, white college-educated geeks far removed from their own congressional districts? Do they know that the vast majority of Black voters who elected them are accounted for in the much larger population of African Americans who regularly access the Internet, approximately 20 million strong? Will they come to understand that the Black netroots community is presently a slumbering giant who, it seems, only the likes of a Fox News Channel can begin to awaken?"[3]

The case of the Jena Six crystallized the development of infrastructure and power within the black blogosphere. The rising profile and influence of blogs such as Electronic Village, Black-Perspective, African American Political Pundit, Jack and Jill Politics, Afro-Netizen, Pam's House Blend, The Field Negro, and more localized blogs such as Dallas South became a national focal point for media and organizing. When the press did start catching up to the events in Jena, they turned to these bloggers as the experts. The end results of their collective online reporting, analysis, and organizing speak for themselves: hundreds of thousands of dollars raised and hundreds of thousands petitions signed.

Their work also highlighted schisms still present in today's media system, in which issues of race are misunderstood or sidelined by both establishment and progressive media outlets. Many in the black blogosphere were not only angry about the treatment of the Jena Six but also angry at the collective silence of the white progressive media.

As we've outlined, a number of progressive media outlets have driven the technological and reporting shifts transforming media and politics, and many still have a distance to go to incorporate these strategies for maximum impact. But a bigger and potentially more complicated challenge is at hand—one that will force them to reevaluate their role in relation to an influential group of potential new users that has the power to deepen and amplify progressive media's impact. In order to take on this challenge, the progressive media must move beyond "pale, male, and stale."

STRATEGIC OPPORTUNITIES

To reach out to and sustain relationships with so-called minority users, progressive media makers need to move beyond their core white audiences (pale), reach out to women and queer communities (male), and stop being so serious all the time (that is, wonkish, humorless, and stale).

These are not matters of political correctness—they are matters of political clout, democratic representation, and sustainability. Between 2004 and 2008, online political media designed to inform and mobilize these communities has largely been produced by interlinked groups of networked outlets: the black blogosphere, with an active subset known as the "Afrospear";[4] the brown blogosphere, comprised of a varied group of contributors concerned with issues of immigration and prejudice; and the feminist blogosphere, which provides more accessible outlets for a younger generation of women. A number of sites and projects also target progressive youth and less traditional progressive activists via humor, culture, and art.

Second-wave feminists have had their print mainstays, most notably *Ms.* magazine, launched in 1971, and *Off Our Backs*, published since 1970, supplemented by an evolving and often short-lived selection of movement newspapers, magazines, and 'zines. In more recent years, edgier feminist magazines have emerged, ranging from *Bitch* magazine, which takes on pop culture from a feminist point of view, to *Bust* magazine, which incorporates pop culture such as fashion layouts and celebrity interviews, to *Hip Mama*, which addresses motherhood with a political and humorous edge. A similar range of publications—from radical and scrappy to commercial and glossy—address politics, lifestyle, culture, art, and trends related to the concerns of GLBTQQ audiences and others challenging traditional gender roles.

In cities across the country, "ethnic" media are also increasingly popular, informing different communities of color and immigrants. Many of these take the form of local newspapers that both tie together communities and reach out into international diasporas organized around shared language or culture. In addition to commercial publications such as *Jet* and *Ebony*, over the past few years new online ethnic media outlets such as The Root, a Washingtonpost/Newsweek Interactive endeavor focusing on African Americans, have also sprung up. But these publications rarely identify their political stance as "progressive."

While legacy progressive media makers are often far better than the establishment media in acknowledging issues of race and gender inequity, many observers still feel that that the issues and perspectives critical to these communities are too often "ghettoized" by these outlets. Progressive media's reporting and analysis will often focus on national (sometimes local) politics, elections, scandals, economic issues, and corruption without looking through the lens of minority communities or regularly reporting on the issues facing them.

Why is this so important to do? Let's get down to brass tacks. In addition to championing core civil rights values, such communities have been noted as major swing voters in the 2004 and 2008 elections. According to an April 2009 report from the Pew Research Center, "The electorate in last year's presidential election was the most racially and ethnically diverse in U.S. history, with nearly one-in-four votes cast by non-whites. . . . The nation's three biggest minority groups—blacks, Hispanics and Asians—each accounted for unprecedented shares of the presidential vote in 2008." Why the dramatic change? "The unprecedented diversity of the electorate last year was driven by increases both in the number and in the turnout rates of minority eligible voters," Pew notes.[5]

Women have also wielded significant political clout in recent elections—especially single women, who skew younger and less financially secure. "Unmarried women played a pivotal role in making this history and in changing this nation," according to Greenberg Quinlan Rosner Research. "They delivered a stunning 70 to 29 percent margin to Barack Obama and delivered similarly strong margins in races for Congress and the U.S. Senate."[6]

Millennials comprise another swing bloc. "In 2008, 18–29 year olds, now all members of the Millennial generation, voted Democratic by a stunning 66–32 margin," wrote Ruy Teixeira, a political demographer and senior fellow at both the Center for American Progress and the Century Foundation.

> Obama's support among 18–29 year olds was remarkably broad, extending across racial barriers. He carried not just Hispanic 18–29 year olds (76–19) and black 18–29 year olds (95–4) but also white 18–29 year olds (54–44). Obama's

> 10-point advantage among white 18–29 year olds contrasts starkly with his 15 [point] deficit among older whites. Obama's huge overall margin among Millennials contributed mightily to his strong victory this November. Indeed, without 18–29 year olds, Obama's popular vote margin would have been slightly under one percentage point."[7]

"So much for the idea there is nothing distinctly progressive about today's Millennials," writes Teixeira in a related report, "Generation We and the 2008 Election."[8]

But it's not good enough to pay attention to these communities when the election season swings into high gear, or just after a national disaster such as Hurricane Katrina. If progressive media organizations want to inform and activate these communities and ultimately move them to more liberal or progressive stances, producers must provide regular and frequent reporting that interests them, appeals to them, and is about them. And frankly, progressives need to be much more conscious that while they may rest on their laurels because they believe in social justice and equality, their actions sometimes do not match their rhetoric.

"The demographics of this country are changing dramatically," says Larry Irving, a former assistant secretary for communications and information in the Clinton administration, in an interview for a Media Consortium report. "Tech is changing dramatically. The willingness to hear progressive media is increasing dramatically. There is a certain window of time to make something long lasting. Progressives like talking openness, but they like being a club."[9]

Irving, who coined the now-popular phrase "the digital divide," contends, "There is anti-democratic smugness in a democratic community. The reason the term 'media elite' catches hold with people is because that's how they come off. They need to have ways to get non-elites receptive to our message where they don't feel condescended to. The biggest challenge to progressive media:

being honest, intellectually embracing and not walling ourselves off from the millions of people who worry that progressive elites look down on them."

This perspective has business repercussions as well. Many in the progressive media, especially within the legacy media, find themselves with an audience of white, aging males. (One of us—Tracy—has often joked that some progressive magazines should start targeting nursing homes for advertising.) Looking to the future, ethnic communities and young women are huge potential new audiences. If harnessed and communicated with correctly, they could become future sources of income, providing sources for advertising dollars, donations, and subscriptions. What's more, it should be an honor and challenge for the progressive media as a whole to be more inclusive and representative of the complicated, messy, and wonderful melting pot known as America.

In "A Party in Search of a Notion," a 2006 article by Michael Tomasky, then the editor of the *American Prospect*, called for the Democrats to turn their back on "the million-little-pieces, interest-group approach to politics," and adopt the philosophy "that citizens should be called upon to look beyond their own self-interest and work for a greater common interest."[10] In supporting this argument—which, to be fair, does credit several civil rights victories to those who organized around their own interests—Tomasky cited an honor roll of male politicians, philosophers, journalists, and even bloggers. In doing so he demonstrated a stifling lack of diversity in a widely touted cover piece suggesting that the politics of diversity be scuttled.

The progressive press could learn from the historic failures of the black press. Kevin Weston, director of new media and youth communications at New America Media, a network of more than seven hundred ethnic outlets that also produces original content across several platforms, reflects on how the black press missed the boat in expanding their audience. "In the eighties, the black press was at its height in terms of numbers of papers and financial stability, but all of the black establishment ignored hip-hop," he says. "*Ebony* didn't put a rapper on its cover until the late '90s. So all of those journalists that would have started in the black press got started in the hip-hop press. Fast-forward to 2009. The black press is still working: it's niche, hyperlocal, and [has] long-time relationships with big advertisers. But they missed out on a whole generation of journalists."

The same could be said for the legacy progressive outlets, and even the most visible members of the blogosphere. Their inability to reach out to a diverse base of contributors and readers has left a gap in political communication, alienating audiences that might otherwise be inclined to identify as progressives. Steve Katz, vice president of strategy and development at *Mother Jones*, echoed Weston's sentiment at a 2005 Media Consortium meeting. "We're trying to redefine who we are to reach the audience of the 21st century," he said. "Progressive media is to the progressive audience as classic rock is to the radio audience. We know we can do better and we know people are looking for good journalism and a progressive point of view."[11]

"Progressive could be a very inclusive term," reflects Weston. "When I was working in the black press, I saw myself as a progressive journalist . . . but the perception is that ["progressive" is] an exclusive term, whiter, older, less hip."

To fill the void, there has been a rise in online communities that have provided compelling and important services for their users. While these online communities often have smaller audience numbers than the more well-known progressive outlets, their function is no less important. These ever-growing media organizations reach targeted communities through a broad set of techniques: reporting and analysis, organizing and action, satire and personal essay, media critique, blogging, and commentary. Like many of the outlets discussed in previous chapters, they provide a safe space for assembling their own choirs: discussing, debating, and assembling around shared concerns. They also provide a critique of both establishment and progressive media, movements, and organizations. Last but not least, they dive more deeply into issues affecting their users.

What often sets these outlets apart is how these producers, sites, and communities reach out and activate their audiences. Their expertise lies in their personal experience, background, and passion, which are reflected in the tone they adopt to communicate with their users—a tone that appeals because it represents an authentic and accessible voice, one that relates a shared identity and experience.

Nezua, one of the most prolific and popular bloggers in the brown blogosphere and founder of the blog The Unapologetic Mexican, points out the schism between the "white" media and the identity-based media. "We're talking about our lives, our families, how our people came to this nation, thinking about our people still in the cross-hairs, seeing hate crimes rise against people like us. We're not coming from a detached, distant, theoretical place. When people exist in the mainstream of power and privilege, they don't have to think about those issues."

Developing an accessible voice is key for any media organization as it balances the cool and measured journalistic or academic approach with the more personal tone that the new media landscape demands. This is also where going beyond "stale" comes in. Alternative and new journalism pioneers—as well as comedians and satirists—set the stage for the rise of Rachel Maddow, Jon Stewart, and Stephen Colbert. Similar approaches are echoed in the more personal style advanced by bloggers, and the rich universe of online humor and culture sites. All of these suggest that a better approach to framing and communicating critical perspectives might lie not in elitist language, as Irving suggests, but in finding more appealing ways to deliver the news. Humor and a willingness to cover and feature pop culture—including sports, music (and while we appreciate Pete Seeger, not that kind of music), television, film, and the miscellaneous trends that inform people's everyday lives—are key ingredients for high-impact progressive media.

MOVING BEYOND PALE

During an August 31, 2006, assembly at Jena High School, a black student asked a teacher if he could sit under a tree that was traditionally a space where only white students gathered. The next day, three nooses dangled from it.

"In response to the three nooses, nearly every Black student in the school stood under the tree in a spontaneous and powerful act of nonviolent protest," recounted Jordan Flaherty in an article almost a year later for *Left Turn*, a small magazine dedicated to reporting on grassroots social justice issues. "The town's district attorney quickly arrived, flanked by police officers, and told the Black students to stop making such a big deal over the nooses, which school officials termed to be a 'harmless prank.' Walters spoke in a school assembly, which like the schoolyard where all of this had begun was divided by race, with the Black students on one side and the white students on the other. Directing his remarks to the Black students, District Attorney Reed Walters said, 'I can make your lives disappear with a stroke of a pen.'"[12]

Despite protests and attempts to discuss the incident, the school board repeatedly rebuffed the parents. The appearance of the nooses was deemed a school prank and the students responsible were given a few days of in-school suspension.

The next few months settled into relative normalcy. Football games were a unifying force. The Jena High team was doing well during the season; two of the leading high scorers during the season were later arrested as members of the Jena Six. But the calm gave way to series of incidents in late November that brought racial tensions to a new height. On November 30 part of the high school was damaged by a fire. Over the course of the weekend, black students were assaulted and threatened; in one incident a white student pulled a shotgun on three black students outside a convenience store.

When school resumed on Monday, six black students beat up a white student who reportedly had ties to the weekend's assaults and was close friends with those who admitted to hanging the nooses. The student was knocked unconscious and taken to the hospital. Despite the fact that he was released several hours later, the black students were quickly charged with attempted second-degree murder and conspiracy, which carry a combined sentence of eighty years. Charges against some of the students were later reduced to aggravated second-degree battery and conspiracy.

Except for local coverage of the event, the national media was silent on this racially charged story for months. *Left Turn* was the first national outlet to focus on Jena with a piece on May 9, 2007.

The article opened with a view of the community response to the arrests of the students, who by now were known as the Jena Six. "Speaking to demonstrators in front of a rural Louisiana courthouse last week, Alan Bean, a Baptist minister from the Texas panhandle, inveighed against injustice. 'The highest crime in the Old Testament,' he declared, 'is to withhold due process from poor people. To manipulate the criminal justice system to the advantage of the powerful, against the poor and the powerless.' As he delivered his message to the crowd, officers from the state police intelligence division watched from the side, videotaping speakers and audience."[13]

Bean, who is white, was actually the impetus for the story hitting the national scene. He sent a few reporters, including Witt of the *Chicago Tribune*, a package of information documenting the facts leading up to the prosecution against the six teenagers. Bean runs Friends of Justice, an organization "that works to uphold due process for all Americans." He first visited Jena in January 2007 and immediately began to scrupulously document all the events leading up to the arrests of the six teenagers. He also began organizing the parents and community to respond. The second time Bean visited Jena, he brought a group of parents to an NAACP office in nearby Baton Rogue, where they were kept waiting for three hours and then told to start a NAACP branch in Jena. "That was a jaw dropper," Bean says.

Bean contacted Witt because of the reporter's previous coverage of the case of Shaquanda Cotton, a black fourteen-year-old girl in Paris, Texas, who was sentenced to up to seven years in prison for pushing a hall monitor.[14] Bean was inspired by Witt's reporting on the Cotton case. "It was not a story about an angel, not a model student. But the disciplinary response was out of proportion to what she had done. What's happening in Jena—you can't excuse their behavior, but you need to put it into context and the overreaction," Bean explains.

Witt's coverage of the Cotton case was pivotal in deepening connections between individual black bloggers, says Shawn Williams, who founded the blog Dallas South in June 2006. Williams grew up in Paris and used his blog to correct the town's effort to whitewash its history and current issues of racism.

Witt says that he knew the Cotton article was good when he wrote it but he didn't expect too much reaction to it. "But within a couple of days I started to get hundreds of e-mails through blogs, places far removed from the *Chicago Tribune*'s Web site. And as I started to figure out where these people were encountering the story, I started to realize there was this network of blogs out there devoted to African American issues that were actually distributing that story. . . . Exactly three weeks after I wrote that initial story, that girl was freed from prison by Texas authorities. And that happened because that story was picked up by these blogs and in turn, triggered this massive petition and letter-writing campaign."[15]

Williams suggests that Witt was actually one of the first reporters to "acknowledge and utilize the power of black bloggers" by sending a link to his first Jena Six article to dozens of them.

The story began to slowly trickle out into the mainstream media and generate one-off mentions among select progressive media organizations. Rick Perlstein wrote a blog post for TomPaine in late June, which was quickly followed by an article by Bill Quigley for Truthout in early July (Bean had also sent Quigley a package of information). On July 10, Amy Goodman and her team at *Democracy Now!* devoted an entire episode to the Jena Six and a week later Goodman did a follow-up in her weekly column.

"*Democracy Now!* was widely credited for shifting the spotlight on the Jena Six from an episode of small town racial injustice to a national battle for civil rights as hundreds of protesters from around the country gathered in Jena to show their support for the arrested teens," reported Julie Crosby, general manager for *Democracy Now!*, in a survey we conducted on progressive media impact. But they were one of only a handful of progressive news organizations that kept their coverage focused on the unfolding saga.

Color of Change became involved around the same time after getting a small number of e-mails from its members. "At the time it sounded not true, like something you would read thirty or forty years ago. I kept asking myself, 'Where's the thing that will make this unravel?'" Rucker reflects. At the time, Color of Change had a hundred thousand members on its e-mail list, and Rucker was convinced that the story of the Jena Six story had the all the makings of a strong online campaign. He was right. Color of Change reached out to their regional list, which helped spark a protest of more than three hundred people (huge for a town of three thousand). In partnership with others, they were able to deliver a petition with forty thousand signatures to the district attorney's office.[16]

The Jena Six were also the ongoing connective tissue for a

loose network within the black blogosphere known as the "Afrospear," defined as a "collective of Black bloggers from around the world who convene online to discuss, strategize, and develop solutions to national and international problems affecting people of the African Diaspora."[17]

One of the major coordinated events that the Afrospear works

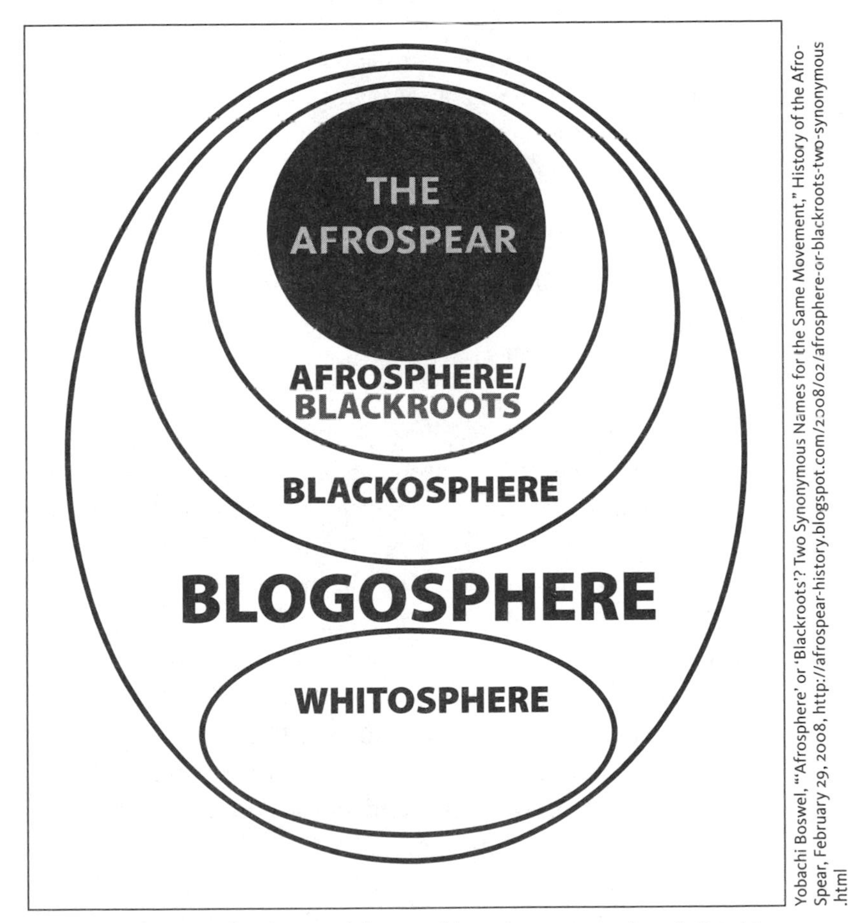

Yobachi Boswel, "'Afrosphere' or 'Blackroots'? Two Synonymous Names for the Same Movement," History of the Afro-Spear, February 29, 2008, http://afrospear-history.blogspot.com/2008/02/afrosphere-or-blackroots-two-synonymous.html

Blogger Francis L. Holland created this graphic to demonstrate the relationship of the Afrospear to other active political blogospheres in 2007.

on is the Day of Blogging for Justice, where many within the black blogosphere come together to highlight an issue that affects the community and call for action.

On August 30, 2007, black bloggers used the Day of Blogging for Justice to highlight the Jena Six. "I want to ask you up front to please call, email or postal mail the national media to urge them to cover this story," wrote Yobachi Boswell of BlackPerspective to his community. He offered his readers strong language from a letter he had written to Governor Kathleen Blanco's office: "Sitting by idle, watching these racial abuses transpire [and] declaring this to be a local issue will only put you in company with many southern governors of times gone by." [18]

"There was not necessarily an infrastructure on the same level before Jena," says Cheryl Contee, who blogs under the handle "Jill Tubman" at Jack and Jill Politics. "It was really coming together and being mutually supportive and developing a stronger bond to groups like Color of Change. We came together during Jena Six and that has been sustained."

While the black blogosphere coalesced, the bloggers united around not only the unjust sentencing of the Jena Six but also what they criticized as a lack of consistent attention by the "white" media to the unfolding events in Jena. When the mainstream media did finally pay attention, specifically in the lead-up to the September 20 march, you could find the AP and major newspapers and networks in Jena. But there was just as much criticism of the coverage by progressive media. On the day that tens of thousands of people traveled to Jena, Pam Spaulding of Pam's House Blend and Chris Kromm of Facing South, a blog for the Institute of Southern Studies, took the progressive blogosphere to task on their silence. Kromm (who's white) wrote:

> But on this historic day for the most high-profile civil rights issue of the moment, where is the progressive blogosphere? I did a quick tour of the major "progressive" sites to see how

> they were covering it—and was astounded to find a complete white-out of this historic cause:
>
> - Daily Kos features a handful of posts about injustice in Iraq today—but not a single entry on its main page, or even its user-generated "diaries," about this important case.
> - Talking Points Memo, a favorite of the DC wonk set, is similarly incensed about foreign policy, but apparently not about racial justice in the South—nothing there either.
> - Long-time progressive blogger Atrios doesn't have a lot of posts up, but found time to touch on Paul Krugman, Iraq and the state of the Euro—but not this major issue.
> - Surely TalkLeft—which has positioned itself as the leading progressive blog about criminal justice issues—would have something? Think again—not a single mention, not even in the quick news briefs!
> - What about another progressive favorite, FireDogLake? A rant about Republicans being "little bitches," but nothing on the Jena 6.
>
> When the Jena 6 does make an appearance on progressive blogs today, it's little more than a passing nod. Huffington Post has a blog post buried below the fold; ThinkProgress gives it a two-sentence news brief.[19]

Spaulding added to Kromm's post with her own theories of why there was such silence.

> "It's not my area of expertise." This is an old saw used to avoid discussing race—it's uncomfortable for white folks and they want to avoid land mines. The easiest way to do that is to say nothing at all, which still speaks volumes. Just about anything can be viewed through the prism of race; in this

> case it's not solely about race, the story of the Jena 6 is about our system of justice and how it can be affected by color, class, power structure, and the almighty dollar.
>
> "It's not my issue": Sorry to say, this gets reinforced by the professional race-ba[i]ting, blacker-than-thou crowd such as Jesse Jackson, who chastised Barack Obama for "acting white" on the issue. That only makes otherwise supportive whites further paranoid. The "black enough" nonsense is divisive and so reflective of old-school mentality often seen in the establishment civil rights set still clinging to power. Of course then Jackson and his ilk will then criticize the lack of diversity in the group of marchers. It's a self-fulfilling prophecy.[20]

Kromm's and Spaulding's posts sparked a firestorm of debate and fury on sites such as Daily Kos and prompted responses from Hamsher of FDL, who said she had someone slated to cover the event, but that person did not make it. Even so, it pointed to the perception by the black blogosphere and its community that the "white" press was not interested in issues critical to the black community. It also brought up the limitations of segregated communication, whether it's among whites or blacks.

Williams agrees that more connections need to be built between the black blogosphere and the white progressive bloggers. "A lot of time the liberal blogosphere say they are open to everyone and don't need to discuss race. They say even if America is not post-racial, the progressive blogosphere is, so we don't need to go down that road internally. If there is going to be a closing in the gap, there has to be more conversation."

This strong message carries even more weight as national demographics change, multiethnic identity becomes increasingly common, and whites no longer hold majority status in many parts of the country. The progressive media has a lot of work to do if it hopes to offer consistent coverage of issues of race, civil rights, and immigration. This means that existing outlets must listen to and work with other outlets that are already doing this critical work, including members of the black and brown blogospheres, magazines such as *ColorLines*, and organizations such as New America Media.

While many of the more reporting-oriented organizations in the progressive media network might not be interested in coordinating around actions and events, working with such networks is a surefire way to generate stories and bring in new and alternative perspectives on national events.

"There is still a chance with these progressive media organizations, especially those that are geographically well-placed with access to young people and ethnic communities like New York or San Francisco to manufacture diversity, to start the process," reflects Weston. "I think that the folks that do it will be better off, and those who don't will have to deal with the demographic realities." In other words: adapt to the multicultural future or fade into irrelevancy.

MOVING BEYOND MALE

But diving deep into issues of race is only one piece of the equation. Women have long found both mainstream and progressive media outlets unfriendly environments for not just feminist discussions but political reporting in general. Overrepresented in journalism school, women dominate feature and lifestyle sections but lag behind on the front page, the editorial pages, and the Sunday shows. Female reporters and editors gather regularly in listservs and at media conferences such as Women, Action & the Media (WAM!) to try to puzzle through why they still feel shut out despite major gains over the last decade. A similar conversation has happened online, with feminist bloggers confronting popular progressive bloggers about their lack of attention to issues of gender and sexual preference.

In the progressive sector, the problem is no longer a lack of role models or leaders. By 2008, several major progressive outlets were led by women: Katrina vanden Heuvel at *The Nation*, Arianna Huffington at the Huffington Post, Joan Walsh at *Salon*, Monika Bauerlein and Clara Jeffery at *Mother Jones*, Amy Goodman at *Democracy Now!*, and more. Reporters and commentators such as Naomi Klein, Amy Sullivan, Katha Pollitt, Barbara Ehrenreich, Laura Flanders, Melissa Harris-Lacewell, and Michelle Goldberg have built high-profile, multiplatform careers and are widely regarded as progressive authorities. Highly visible personalities such as Janeane Garofalo and Ana Marie Cox have set a new tone for female commentators: acerbic, quick, and ready to go toe to toe with the "boy bloggers" that dominate the scene. And Rachel Maddow is the dream anchor for this generation of feminists: a smart, funny, deeply thoughtful host—and a lesbian to boot—who makes a habit of bringing on other women and actually giving them uninterrupted airtime to express their thoughts.

Still, all of this has not yet translated into equal representation. In a 2006 article, "The Byline Gender Gap," Ann Friedman—deputy editor at the *American Prospect*—tallied the damage:

> Conventional wisdom among many women journalists (and their male allies) is that change will come when more women rise to positions of editorial power—which just hasn't happened. Certainly magazines should take steps to elevate competent women not just to the editor-in-chief level, but to all gatekeeper editorial positions. But I don't think the mere presence of female editors can remedy the byline gender gap. Several national and progressive magazines have female editors-in-chief, but you wouldn't know it by looking at each table of contents. There are countless days when all of the progressive news websites feature only one or two stories by women. I know these are places where the editors would agree that the paucity of female bylines is a problem.

She goes on to provide a count of male to female names on the masthead at various outlets from that period:[21]

The American Prospect	21:12
The Atlantic	27:6
Harper's Magazine	30:2 (masthead not online)
In These Times	6:6
Mother Jones	10:5
The New Yorker	44:18
The Nation	26:4
The New Republic	12:2
Salon	14:7
Slate	20:6
Washington Monthly	30:5

What gives? There is a running debate about what holds female political reporters and editors back: typecasting, patriarchy, shyness, a biologically driven distaste for the combative and dualistic tone of many political debates. And there's always the question of what constitutes legitimate news. "My experience is that an awful lot of straight male editors do not see anything related to the reproductive organs as a serious public policy issue," E.J. Graff, the co-author of *Getting Even: Why Women Still Don't Get Paid Like Men and What to Do About It*, told one of us for a 2005 *In These Times* piece on the byline gap. "Unfortunately, those magazines help set the public policy agenda for the country."[22]

In the run-up to the 2008 presidential election, the presence of both a female candidate and a black candidate did help to diversify bylines and media appearances for a time. But "campaign coverage is a very specific type of breaking-news, breaking-scandal,

24/7 media, which is not a style of journalism that is particularly friendly to women and people of color—those environments tend to be very clubby and dude-heavy," says Friedman. She notes that she saw fewer of these voices in the opinion sphere as news of the economic meltdown began to dominate. "Also, early Obama administration reporting has come largely from seasoned DC reporters, who are predominantly white and male," she notes, "and even the new press corps additions—see Sam Stein of HuffPo—are *still* white dudes." Friedman explains that she's tried to balance things out in the *American Prospect* by not segregating women's issues from other political coverage, and by encouraging writers to "discuss how what they're covering interacts with issues of class/gender/race, even if that's not part of the thesis." She credits *In These Times* and AlterNet for regularly including women, but notes that "by and large, even the progressive publications that are headed by women (*Mother Jones*, *The Nation*) have seriously white/male tables of contents."

Mother Jones has done some catching up since 2006, adding more women to their reporting roster. "I'm sure some of it has to do with the fact that there has been, for a long time, two women here doing a lot of the story assigning, and it's obviously something we care about," said Jeffery in a 2007 interview with Dana Goldstein on the Campus Progress blog. "I do think that the issue of why women don't get bylines at major magazines is a complicated one. It's a combination of actual sexism with real issues having to do with women leaving the workforce for a while to raise their kids. When they're writers, they come back and write about those issues, and perhaps not others. All we know is that we want more women, not just at our magazine, but in every magazine."[23]

They may still have to wait a while before the numbers match up. Even newer networked progressive media outlets suffer from the dreaded dude-fest disorder. "Current and former TPM staffers have spoken of a grueling pace, constant pressures for content, and strict enforcement from the site's managing editor, a former

TPM commenter and lawyer based in Missouri," reported *Politico*'s Michael Calderone in a May 2009 piece. "The work environment has been described as a 'boy's club,' and indeed, several women have left TPM after working there for just a few months."[24] While TPM editors note that turnover has been common among staffers of both genders, the perception lingers.

In the meantime, feminist outlets serve as both a training ground and a safe space for rising female political writers. One of the most popular progressive blogs in this vein is Feministing, edited by Jessica Valenti and a team of female editors and contributors, including Friedman. The site, founded in mid-2004, was designed explicitly to provide a platform for younger women to "speak on their own behalf on issues that affect their lives and futures. Feministing provides a platform for us to comment, analyze, influence and connect."[25]

Valenti has made a career out of writing about and for the rising generation of women that still proudly call themselves feminists, despite many efforts to pronounce the movement dead. She's penned three related books: *Full Frontal Feminism: A Young Woman's Guide to Why Feminism Matters* (2007), *He's a Stud, She's a Slut, and 49 Other Double Standards Every Woman Should Know* (2008), and *The Purity Myth: How America's Obsession with Virginity Is Hurting Young Women* (2009), all published by Seal Press, an independent publishing house dedicated to producing edgy books "by women and for women."

The site has mobilized its audience around campaigns to hold media and commercial outlets accountable. Valenti recounts several moments of impact between 2004 and 2008:

- Feministing writers lobbied against Wal-Mart for selling girls' underwear that read "Who Needs Credit Cards?" They were joined in this campaign by conservative media commentators, and the product was pulled from the shelves.

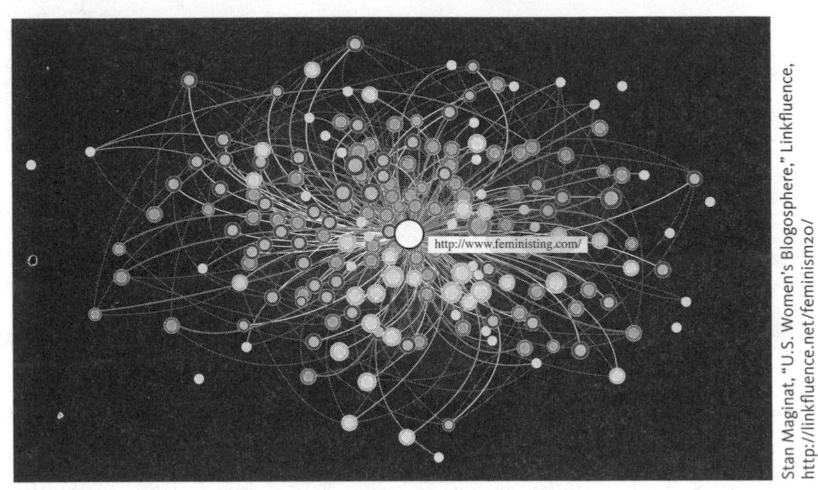

Stan Maginat, "U.S. Women's Blogosphere," Linkfluence, http://linkfluence.net/feminism20/

In early 2009, Linkfluence unveiled a map of the top thirty blogs within the feminist blogosphere. Feministing was ranked the most influential based on the number of incoming links to the site.

- The site spearheaded a successful campaign to remove a T-shirt reading "No Means No Unless I'm Drunk" from the catalog of the David and Goliath company.
- Feministing writers persuaded *Time* magazine to print a retraction of an article defining the morning-after pill as "abortion inducing."

The site has been instrumental in both reframing feminist issues for a new generation of readers and activists and broadening the choir for progressive issues by attracting young female readers and contributors. As a December 2006 article from *Marie Claire* notes: "Feminism is fun again! Every bit as edifying as your women's studies books from college, but with a biting sense of humor that keeps things punchy, not preachy." Feministing has been profiled in the *New York Times*, *The Guardian*, *Elle*, and *Salon*. Valenti appeared on *The Colbert Report* to speak about her first book, *Full*

Frontal Feminism. Valenti and other Feministing bloggers regularly speak at university campuses around the country.

Not only has Feministing mobilized a unique, younger audience by merging pop culture and politics, but Valenti and her colleagues have become leaders in what is now a vibrant feminist blogosphere. At the 2009 Fem 2.0 conference, social media mapping company Linkfluence offered a visualization of the feminist blogosphere, and Feministing was ranked the most influential based on the number of incoming links to the site.[26]

What's more, the site is noted as influential within the progressive media sector in a 2008 analysis by the same company:

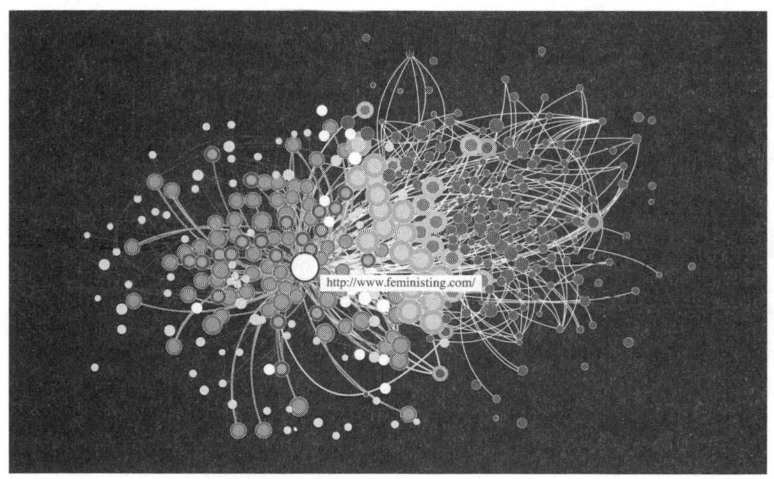

Stan Maginat, "Presidential Watch 08," Linkfluence, http://presidentialwatch08.com/index.php/map/

In a 2008 analysis, Linkfluence mapped out the dozens of influential progressive, independent and conservative blogs..

Friedman notes that there were some criticisms of this analysis, since not all bloggers who write about women's issues use and identify with the term "feminism," especially sites run by bloggers of color. They saw this as "a skewed, white-dominated map that betrays the level of diversity in the feminist blogosphere," she said.

Such racial politics within feminism have been a tense issue since the movement's first wave, and continue to cause friction.

Shireen Mitchell, the chair of the Media and Technology Task Force of the National Council of Women's Organizations, worked with Linkfluence to develop the map, and notes the limitations of such data-driven analysis. Many female bloggers of color prefer terms such as "womanist," a word coined by Alice Walker in the early 1980s to distinguish the concerns and experiences of black women who found white feminism exclusionary. By centering this analysis on the term "feminist," the Linkfluence map reinscribes that exclusion. "Who decides what is and isn't relevant conversations?" wrote "Renee" of Womanist Musings, the only single-author blog run by a woman of color that appeared on the Fem 2.0 list.

> If a womanist blogger decides that her primary focus is race and how it [a]ffects her life, does that suddenly make her less feminist? I believe that considering that feminism has a history of silencing WOC [women of color] when we dare to speak about the ways in which race effects our life, this is an extremely important question to ask.
>
> WOC have routinely called upon white feminists to not only share their space but give considered thought to what we have to say. I have held fast to the desire for openness by making my space open to those who identify as feminist/womanist across race, class and gender lines. This is not something that has been replicated across the blogosphere. To say it plainly, when we speak out about racism what we receive is backlash.[27]

Mitchell agrees that there is still progress to be made in bridging these communities. "It's a very divisive conversation," she says, one which also relates to issues of class and social justice. She notes that the term "progressive" also carries the connotation of white privilege. As an example, she notes that conversations around equal pay often use a statistic—77 cents on the dollar—that represents white women's salaries. Black women earn only 72 cents on average, and Latino women 60 cents. "The assumption is that if this moves, it'll move for everyone else," she says. "But if you make it there, are you going to come back to fight for it? That's where the line is."

Mindful of such schisms, Feministing's authors have worked to provide new avenues of visibility for other women interested in feminist issues, whatever they label themselves. In 2008, the editors redesigned the blog to emphasize community participation and serve as a platform for women's rights organizations, especially those serving the GLBTQQ community and communities of color. They created community diaries that are streamed into their own feed, with recommended posts that Feministing editors promote to the front page of the site. These have attracted contributors ranging from the ACLU to a fourteen-year-old girl. "It's been really wonderful because we have a real diversity of people posting on the site," says Valenti. "The whole idea of starting Feministing was to create a platform for young women who didn't have their voices heard; we felt like we have our platform and wanted to give one to other people."

The community contributors have gotten noticed; one diarist with no professional journalism training got a clip in the *Toronto Star* on the basis of a post she wrote about Susan Boyle, the singing sensation whose appearance on *Britan's Got Talent* became a viral hit.

Traffic has doubled since they put the community blogs up in mid-2008—a year later, the site was attracting half a million unique readers a month, according to Valenti. She estimates from reader surveys that most of those readers are young women, largely in the United States but also in the United Kingdom, Australia, and India. Their largest group of readers were age ten to twenty-six—a prime demographic for graying progressive outlets.

Valenti says the site is unique in that they occupy a middle ground—not academic, not long-form feminist philosophy. They develop personalities on the blog, and do in-person outreach, such as happy hours in New York and Los Angeles. "People feel like they know us," she says. "They feel like we're friends, and sometimes we are."

Valenti says she's collaborated occasionally with legacy progressive outlets, writing for *The Nation*, *In These Times*, and TAPPED (the blog of the *American Prospect*), but there are more opportunities for growth. "I would love to see more kickass women with personality becoming the house bloggers at sites like the *The Atlantic* or the *The Nation*. That would certainly be a draw for younger women," Valenti says. "Why do younger women want to sit around reading a bunch of dudes who dismiss their issues?" In the progressive blogosphere, she says, she's now "familiar enough with the boys that if I ask them to post something they will . . . but I think that Feministing is derided in some circles because we've been granted some access." Also, Valenti notes, it's too easy for them to link to Feministing and think, "'We've done our feminist work for the day.' I wish they'd be working through a feminist lens, not just throwing up a few links to get their feminist cookie."

BEYOND STALE

Britney! Paris! Will Brangelina adopt another baby?

So, are these the subjects you have to talk about to get beyond stale? Well, yes . . . and no. But progressive media outlets do need to learn how to interact with popular culture on a more authentic and, frankly, less snobby level.

Many of the outlets noted above attract a different demographic because they speak a language that's casual and laced with references to pop culture figures and trends. They take the issues that affect younger progressives seriously, but they don't feel like they need to adopt a serious tone for everything. They can talk about their favorite hit movies, but also dissect them through a political lens. Users identify with the sites and contributors because they feel they share the same world.

Weston, who operates New America Media's YO! Youth Outlook—a successful youth media project that includes a print publication, a radio show, a cable show, and online multimedia content—says that the only way to produce media that will interest younger users is to involve them in producing it. He criticizes media projects that see younger contributors only as interns or free labor.

"It's not a done deal that you bring in young people and you go from being *The Nation* to being MTV," he says, but once you do it, "you're showing your respect to that generation's voice, and you'd be guided by them in terms of editorial direction, what actual stories you should be working on. . . . When you invest in young people you can make a smaller investment that goes a longer way. But most news organizations just aren't willing to bring young people in or don't know how."

Both legacy and emerging progressive outlets will also need to come to terms with the shift in tone preferred by Generation X and millennial audiences. While *The Daily Show* and *The Colbert Report* do not explicitly define themselves as "progressive," their ironic take on politics and current affairs has shaped the tone for news coverage across the media landscape.

In *The New Blue Media*, Theodore Hamm identifies three different and long-standing styles of political communication: satirical, didactic, and activist. The satirical mode of communication spiked in popularity during the Bush years, when so many mainstream sources reported straight-faced on news that many of us found absolutely unbelievable. Just as ethnic and feminist media sources provide an authentic voice for their communities, the ironic approach mirrored the voices in many of our heads. As a result, the comedy shows quickly became serious news.

"Political humorists . . . serve up truth in the guise of Colbert's 'truthiness.' Rather than foster debilitating cynicism, these comedians-cum-newscasters reflect a contemporary mode of communication in which irony is not antithetical to—but synonymous with—authenticity," wrote Jessica in her 2006 *In These Times* piece titled "In Politics, Comedy Is Central." "We have moved beyond the much-heralded (and lamented) GenX cynicism of the late '90s. Sarcasm, doubt and distance have become default positions, havens in a world of fundamentalisms, false promises and lies."[28]

Playful, creative approaches to political communication also often trump the stale critiques and lamentations that fill much of legacy progressive media. In his 2007 book *Dream: Re-imagining Progressive Politics in an Age of Fantasy*, professor and activist Stephen Duncombe lays out a new blueprint for activists and media makers:

> For years progressives have comforted themselves with age-old biblical adages that the "truth will out" or "the truth shall make you free." We abide by an Enlightenment faith that somehow, if reasoning people have access to the Truth, the scales will fall from their eyes and they will see reality as it truly is and, of course, agree with us. But waiting around for the truth to set people free is lazy politics.
>
> The truth does not reveal itself by virtue of being the truth: it must be told, and we need to learn how to tell the truth more effectively. It must have stories woven around it, works of art made about it; it must be communicated in new ways and marketed so that it sells. It must be embedded in an experience that connects with people's dreams and desires, that resonates with the symbols and myths they find meaningful. We need a propaganda of the truth.
>
> Progressives like to study and to know. We like to be right (and then complain that others are not). But being right is

> not enough—we need to win. And to win we need to act. I propose an alternative political aesthetic for progressives to consider, a theory of dreampolitik they might practice.[29]

This "dreampolitik" includes learning lessons from pop culture about how to engage, move, and transform users. Duncombe drew from such varied sources as the video game *Grand Theft Auto*, the grassroots activist gathering Reclaim the Streets, and the lessons of Madison Avenue to suggest new tools and forms of communication and outreach. "Modern politics is about appealing to people; you need to attract activists into an organization and supporters to your cause. The hair shirt wearing, self-sacrificing progressive may be a suitable candidate for sainthood, but politically they are a liability. Branding is the new buzzword in advertising; it's the set of associations attached to a product or corporation. Politics, whether we like it or not, are branded too. The important question is what sort of brand we want to build," he wrote.

The networked communications platforms that have arisen even since Duncombe wrote this make it many times easier to build not only powerful brands but strong, effective networks. Linking those networks—the pale, the stale, the brown, the black, the female, the male, and everyone in between—around issues, elections, legislation, and more is the route to high-impact progressive media.

SECTION III:
MOVING FORWARD

WHAT NEXT?

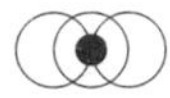

The first hundred days of the Obama administration represented a political shift nearly as dramatic as the post-9/11 moment that shaped the Bush administration and spawned the growth of the progressive media network.

The election of a black man to the highest office in the land confounded assumptions about American's racial prejudices. The seesawing economy unseated long-standing analysis of our financial system, and discredited conservative truisms about the "free market." The candidate himself related to both mainstream and new media in a very different way than his predecessor had—openly supporting government transparency and talking directly to smaller outlets and citizen journalists.[1] Major newspapers began to shut down, undone by both new business models and their own inability to retain the loyalty of their disillusioned readers. Progressive media makers and pundits found themselves alternately charmed and unsettled by their redefined relationship to this president, who spoke a new language of bipartisanship, shared sacrifice, and rational deliberation.

What's more, he seemed to actually understand and value the importance of a vigorously critical media. As Obama said at the 2009 White House Correspondents Dinner, "I may not agree with everything you write or report. I may even complain . . . from time to time about how you do your jobs, but I do so with the knowledge that when you are at your best, then you help me be at my best. You help all of us who serve at the pleasure of the American people do our jobs better by holding us accountable, by demanding honesty, by preventing us from taking shortcuts and falling into easy political games that people are so desperately weary of. And that kind of reporting is worth preserving—not just for your sake, but for the public's."

How can the strategies defined above, which had begun to work well for progressives over the last eight years, help them to continue to make an impact in this new reality? Progressive media makers need to consider what mission-driven strategies will help them to secure buzz, influence, and credibility during this next cycle, and to continue to engage with users and expand their base.

In order to increase their impact, they need to embrace a few new goals. They need to resist the impulse to return to sectarian battles now that the unifying power of anti-Bush sentiment is no longer the driving force for progressives. Continuing to assemble and inspire the progressive choir will require outlets and producers to express vision and political savvy rather than just partisan ire. Members of the progressive media sector also need to make sure that they aren't co-opted by the Obama administration and the Democratic Congress, now in power, instead holding politicians' feet to the fire, watching for broken promises, compromises, and corruption on both sides of the aisle. With increasing government transparency, the role of the progressive media may also shift from digging for data and documents to analyzing, contextualizing, and sifting through them for meaning.

To meet these new goals, here's our advice for how progressive media makers can evolve and adapt the strategies described in Section II.

STRENGTHEN THE NETWORK-POWERED MEDIA SYSTEM

This is not the time, politically or strategically, to work in a silo. Now that the various layers of networks have been established, they will only deepen and grow. It's important to strategically integrate network layers (networked individuals, self-organizing networks, institutional networks, and networks of institutions) for maximum impact. It's time to step up and build connections with key partners—whether this is your community of users, other outlets, or allied institutions. Collaboration is one of the major new routes to success.

More and more, journalism organizations are taking advantage of social media platforms to involve users by providing the information, motivation, and tools to participate in public affairs issues and related online/offline communities. Frequently these are distributed, rather than native to the outlets' sites. During early 2009, Twitter broke out of the pack as a flexible and highly influential platform for journalists and newsmakers (not to mention Ashton Kutcher) to communicate with readers, sources, and one another. But that's just one example—there are many tools to try and new ones emerging all the time. Don't be afraid to open up, to play, to authentically connect.

Formalized media networks, such as The Media Consortium, and informal networks of blogs and activists must find the best options to work together. Their work must also be supported by funders and individuals to drive innovation, testing, and incubation of projects that lead progressive media organizations into the twenty-first century. This is going to require time to explore new business models, experiment with mobile media (from phones to the Kindle), and to train media outlets and producers to learn about and integrate new reporting practices such as citizen journalism.

KEEP TELLING THE RIGHT THEY'RE WRONG

This is not the role for every outlet, but it has proven to be a high-impact strategy with tangible outcomes for many within the progressive media network. It's important to stay vigilant even when no election is in sight—conservatives weren't happy about losing and began to organize immediately after the election to build their own networked infrastructure.

Besides, it's fun—what could be more mockable than the sight of Fox's Glenn Beck weeping multiple times in the early weeks of the Obama administration? As Jon Stewart noted, "For God's sake, guys. You've been out of power for ten f*%#ng weeks. You've got a mid-term election in twenty months. Pace your rage!"[2] Fat chance—the right is relentless. Keep the pressure on.

For example, Rush Limbaugh became a particular target in early 2009 as a result of his remarks at the Conservative Political Action Conference that he hoped Obama would fail—a flap that drove the news cycle for a week and gave progressive commentators tremendous amounts of material to mock, distribute, and amplify.

Keys to success for this strategy include:

1. Communicate facts and reporting through accessible, spreadable, and visual means. This helps content go viral.

2. Don't wait for the right to attack—identify and create proactive campaigns that will drive the news cycle.

3. Last but not least, don't be afraid to "poke the bear" when appropriate—i.e., go after the likes of O'Reilly, Limbaugh, or a corporate target. Their egos can't take it and they are sure to respond—and will misconstrue remarks, defame people, and prod their audiences to respond with venom. But with that warning in mind, you can take advantage of the fact that such a response can heighten the public awareness around your work.

MAXIMIZE MUCKRAKING WITH USER INVOLVEMENT

In a networked media environment it is critical to bring your users into the investigative mix. You can generate new citizen journalism initiatives such as the models exemplified by Talking Points Memo, Off the Bus, and The Uptake.

At the very least, you will need to allow your users to play. What do we mean? It's time to loosen up control on your content and offer opportunities for your users to get involved in story generation, creation, and dissemination. Bring them into the story planning process. Allow them to help gather resources, relevant articles, interviews, and more that can be integrated into the final product and as extras. This will result in much more buy-in, both in terms of your journalism and in terms of users participating, donating, and disseminating the content to their networks, friends, and family.

Move from single stories to more context-driven media products. The bigger outlets are producing dozens of single articles, videos, and radio spots on a topic every day. Many are driven by the news cycle, which means that single stories run the risk of attracting just their fifteen minutes of fame (or more often not attracting it) and then disappearing. But over time, many individual small pieces can all add up to an overall story, providing broader context and meaning. Offer users such content in a wide range of formats, from visuals to databases to widgets and beyond.

There are no magic bullets. Don't forget that investigation always requires skill, training, and money. The networked media environment may demand extra resources for new skills, including the hybrid role of a community manager/editor, who can work with the community and also have the news sense to direct and support a project.

But don't despair if an investigation seems long, intricate, or arcane; focus on the impact it can make. The muckraking projects described in the chapters above yielded yet more results in the Obama administration's first one hundred days. Karl Rove was called to testify in front of Congress on the U.S. attorneys firing scandal. Marcy Wheeler of Firedoglake scrutinized Justice Department memos, revealing that enemy combatant Khalid Sheikh Mohammed had been waterboarded 183 times in one month. Her scoop was picked up and amplified by the *New York Times*, sparking a nationwide debate and calls for a special prosecutor.

Watch for new projects, such as the Huffington Post Investigative Fund, launched in 2009, to continue to push the evolution of muckraking. Their motto: "Report once, run anywhere."

TAKE A POLICY STANCE . . . AND DON'T RETREAT

Journalists, don't be afraid to pick a side on an issue and champion it. Ari Melber, who both covered and participated in the Get FISA Right campaign described earlier, notes that one of the most valuable early contributions of Glenn Greenwald on the issue was just covering the topic in depth, "reporting it out with a perspective." For his work, Greenwald received the Izzy Award in 2009, named after the much-respected independent reporter I. F. Stone.

Melber also observes that while print journalists often feel compelled to cover issues from multiple sides, outlets such as Keith Olbermann's show allow guests to champion and articulate a single perspective. You have to define "what do you want to be, and what you are comfortable doing in the place of impact," he says. "The idea that someone reports something and it will fix itself no longer applies."

Outlets, it's also important for you to let activists and bloggers know if you are covering a simmering issue that's tied to a legislative battle. Jon Pincus, who organized the Get FISA right campaign, also acknowledges that the campaign could have been strengthened and humanized by the addition of more narrative coverage of the issue. Transparency with your audience is key to developing and maintaining credibility. Be honest with your audience about your orientation to a policy or issue. Invite them to keep you or your organization accountable as you deliver high-quality and high-impact reporting.

New platforms for communicating about legislative campaigns can draw mainstream coverage. It's important to understand the impact that different platforms can deliver. For example, Melber says, it meant something different for activists who already supported Obama to organize on the candidate's social network, MyBarackObama, than it did for them to organize on the transition platform, Change.gov. "If you criticize someone in church, it's different if you say it to a congregant outside or to a newspaper," says Melber, who in 2009 helped to craft yet another social media platform designed to connect citizens with lawmakers, the People's Press Conference.

HELP THE CHOIR BECOME CONDUCTORS

Don Tapscott, author of the books *Wikinomics* and *Grown Up Digital*, says, "Publishers need to think of themselves not as publishers, but as community builders."[3] But what does that mean? Media outlets and makers will need to consult their users and their own strategic goals to figure out what kind of communities they want to build, how to connect them, and how to move them.

As noted, the progressive choir is not one monolithic group that is already singing the same tune. The progressive choir is a wildly diverse community that engages in constant debate and brings differing viewpoints into the mix. The art is actually assembling the choir to take action. Choir building starts with regular interaction between media producers and users. (Note: Interaction does not mean e-mail blasts with a digital signature.) It's going to mean diving into the weeds, being willing to hear feedback, ideas, and questions—and responding.

Once your choir is relatively established, the next step is to move them to actions, large and small: fund-raising, volunteering, petitioning, voting, recruiting and more. Although many blogs are incorporating more reporting practices into their daily routine, they are still not bound by the rules that traditional journalism-oriented organizations hold themselves to. Many traditional outlets are in a tough spot. They do not feel it is their role or duty to advocate for particular actions for their users. At the same time, in order to fulfill their social mission and document their impact, it is critical to demonstrate how users are benefiting from and utilizing the information they provide.

What about a compromise? Offer the space for your audiences to self-organize. Take a page from the Obama playbook, Facebook, and Twitter and allow your users to harness media to activate themselves and their networks. Instead of just letting them comment on articles, help them to create groups to do something with what they've learned.

D.I.Y.

Feeling marginalized? Start a blog, join a social network, be heard. Feeling stale and gray? Reach out to new networks and communities. Work with musicians, artists, fashion designers—spice things up.

The boundaries that marked older forms of one-to-many communication are dissolving, and the power of previous gatekeepers is waning. The sky is the limit for authentic, amusing, moving, creative progressive media production. Remember, *you* are the future of progressive media. As Markos Moulitsas said in a May 2009 interview, "The broader netroots—and to me it's one big interconnected ecosystem—has become integral. It's going to be the key way, moving forward, that people use to communicate."[4]

Opportunities for creating diverse, connected, progressive media are always blooming. In early 2009, organizers from the Color of Change and the Video the Vote projects joined together to form the Citizen Engagement Lab designed to help communities self-organize, amplify issues, and move to action.[5] But not all projects need to be so elaborate. Pincus describes a Twitter tag, #p2, which was formulated in 2009 to aggregate tweets about diverse content that is—or should be—of interest to networked progressives.

BONUS ROUND: COME UP WITH YOUR OWN STRATEGIES AND TELL US ABOUT THEM

We've done our best to identify the strategies that really worked, but for lack of space, knowledge, or reach, no doubt we've left some out. We've also only been able to focus on a limited number of progressive outlets. Let us know what else is going on out there that makes an impact.

Meanwhile, we'll be continuing to document the evolution of progressive media sector at our blog, beyondtheecho.net.

NOTES

Introduction

1. "Jeremy Scahill Testifies on Defense Contracting," YouTube, May 10, 2007, http://www.youtube.com/watch?v-sdk4dIXqs7s.
2. "Hearing on Defense Contractors: Robert Greenwald's Testimony," YouTube, http://www.youtube.com/watch?v=NYsIC5Jwrhw&feature=related.
3. Jeremy Scahill, "Justice, of a Sort, for Blackwater," *The Nation*, December 8, 2008, http://www.thenation.com/doc/20081222/scahill.
4. Jeremy Scahill, "KBR Got Bonuses for Work That Killed Soldiers," *The Nation*, May 20, 2009, http://www.thenation.com/doc/20090601/scahill.
5. Andrew Garib, "What Is Progressive?" Campus Progress, July 13, 2005, http://www.campusprogress.org/features/384/what-is-progressive.
6. Nate Silver, "The Two Progressivisms," Fivethirtyeight.com, February 15, 2009, http://www.fivethirtyeight.com/2009/02/two-progressivisms.html.
7. Kathleen Hall Jamieson and Joseph N. Cappella, *Echo Chamber: Rush Limbaugh and the Conservative Media Establishment* (New York: Oxford University Press, 2008), 242–44.

1. Setting the Stage for Change

1. "Election Night: A Media Watch Special Report," Online NewsHour, http://www.pbs.org/newshour/media/election2000/election_night.html.
2. Eric Boehlert, *Lapdogs: How the Press Rolled Over for Bush* (New York: Free Press, 2006), 234.
3. Jerome Armstrong and Markos Moulitsas Zuniga, *Crashing the Gate: Net-*

roots, Grassroots and the Rise of People-Powered Politics (White River Junction, VT: Chelsea Green Publishing Company, 2006), 35–36.

4. Lakshmi Chaudhry, “Can Blogs Revolutionize Progressive Politics?” *In These Times*, February 6, 2006, http://www.inthesetimes.com/article/2485.
5. Theodore Hamm, *The New Blue Media: How Michael Moore, MoveOn.org, Jon Stewart and Company Are Transforming Progressive Politics* (New York: The New Press, 2008), 63.
6. David Brock, *The Republican Noise Machine: Right-Wing Media and How It Corrupts Democracy* (New York: Crown Publishing Group, 2004), 3.
7. Robert Borosage, “The Mighty Wurlitzer: What Progressives Can Learn from David Brock’s Account of the Conservative Machine,” *American Prospect*, May 5, 2002, http://www.prospect.org/cs/articles?article=the_mighty_wurlitzer.
8. Hamm, *New Blue Media*, p. xii.
9. Don Hazen, “New Progress for Progressive Media,” AlterNet, April 18, 2006, http://www.alternet.org/media/35074.
10. Stephen Colbert, White House Correspondents Dinner Speech, April 30, 2006, A-Infos Radio Project, http://www.radio4all.net/index.php?op=script&program_id=17953&version_id=20967&nav=series&session=.
11. Zogby International, “Zogby Poll: 67% View Traditional Journalism as ‘Out of Touch,’” February 27, 2008, http://www.zogby.com/news/ReadNews.cfm?ID=1454.
12. Nielsen Wire, “Nov. 2008: U.S. News Sites See Post-Election Growth,” December 24, 2008, http://blog.nielsen.com/nielsenwire/online_mobile/nov-2008-us-news-sites-see-post-election-growth.
13. David Carr and Brian Stelter, “Campaigns in a Web 2.0 World,” *New York Times*, November 2, 2008, http://www.nytimes.com/2008/11/03/business/media/03media.html.
14. Jeff Cohen, “Big Election Winner: Indy Media,” Common Dreams, November 5, 2008, http://www.commondreams.org/view/2008/11/05-8.

2. Networking Your Way to Impact

1. Allison Fine, *Social Citizens* (Washington, DC: Case Foundation, 2008), http://www.scribd.com/doc/2626239/Social-Citizens-Discussion-Paper.
2. Sydney Jones and Susannah Fox, “Generations Online in 2009,” Pew

Internet and American Life Project, January 28, 2009, http://www.pewinternet.org/Reports/2009/Generations-Online-in-2009.aspx.

3. Allen's Listening Tour, August 11, 2006, http://www.youtube.com/watch?v=9G7gq7GQ71c&.
4. "PTVs Top 10: The Greatest Political Web Videos of All Time," You Tube, http://www.youtube.com/watch?v=PcszvVWJTUg.
5. Ari Melber, "YouTubing the Election," *The Nation*, November 4, 2008, http://www.thenation.com/doc/20081117/melber2.
6. Tony Deifell, *The Big Thaw: Charting a New Future for Journalism*, vol. 2 (The Media Consortium, 2009), 24.
7. Henry Jenkins et al., "If It Doesn't Spread, It's Dead (Part Five): Communities of Users," Confessions of an Aca-Fan: The Official Weblog of Henry Jenkins, February 20, 2009, http://henryjenkins.org/2009/02/if_it_doesnt_spread_its_dead_p_4.html.
8. Amy Gahran, interview by Tracy Van Slyke, December 12, 2008.
9. Ari Melber, "Change.Gov's First Big Failure," *The Nation*, January 15, 2009, http://www.thenation.com/blogs/state_of_change/397835/change_gov_s_first_big_failure.
10. Susan Page, "Norquist's Power High, Profile Low," *USA Today*, June 1, 2001, http://www.usatoday.com/news/washington/2001-06-01-grover.htm.
11. Matt Stoller, "The Open Left," MyDD, May 1, 2007, http://www.mydd.com/story/2007/5/1/232437/5390.

3. Why—and How—Progressive Media Matter

1. Bob Ostertag, *People's Movements, People's Press: The Journalism of Social Justice Movements* (Boston: Beacon Press, 2006), 3.
2. Nielsen Media Research, "Anytime Anywhere Media Measurement," 2009, http://www.nielsenmedia.com/nc/portal/site/Public/menuitem.9716da1f5789380e211ba0a347a062a0/?vgnextoid=406ae2b5079bb010VgnVCM100000ac0a260aRCRD.
3. Jay Rosen, "Audience Atomization Overcome: Why the Internet Weakens the Authority of the Press," PressThink, January 12, 2009, http://journalism.nyu.edu/pubzone/weblogs/pressthink/2009/01/12/atomization.html.
4. Linkfluence, "Presidential Watch 2008," http://presidentialwatch08.com/index.php/tag/linkfluence/.
5. Yochai Benkler, "Participation as Sustainable Cooperation in Pursuit

of Public Goals," in *Rebooting America: Ideas for Redesigning American Democracy for the Internet Age*, ed. Micah L. Sifry, Allison Fine, Andrew Rasiej, and Joshua Levy (Washington, DC: Personal Democracy Press, 2008), http://rebooting.personaldemocracy.com, 49–50.

4. Build Network-Powered Media

1. Markos Moulitas, Address, YearlyKos Convention, June 9, 2006, http://www.archive.org/details/yearlykos_markos.
2. Adam Nagourney, "Gathering Highlights Power of the Blog," *New York Times*, June 10, 2006, http://www.nytimes.com/2006/06/10/us/10bloggers.html.
3. Eartha Jane Melzer, "Lose Your House, Lose Your Vote," Michigan Messenger, September 10, 2008, http://michiganmessenger.com/4076/lose-your-house-lose-your-vote.
4. "Save the Internet: Top Ten Examples of Grassroots Mobilization in the Net Neutrality Fight I," MoveOn.org, http://civic.moveon.org/save_the_internet/littleguy.html.
5. Matthew Klam, "Fear and Laptops on the Campaign Trail," *New York Times Magazine*, September 26, 2004, http://www.nytimes.com/2004/09/26/magazine/26BLOGS.html.
6. Matt Stoller, "The Open Left," MyDD, May 1, 2007, http://www.mydd.com/story/2007/5/1/232437/5390.
7. Mark Murray, "First Thoughts: Obamanation's Power," MSNBC.com, http://firstread.msnbc.msn.com/archive/2008/04/18/915576.aspx.
8. Jon Henke, "New Guards," QandO Blog, April 18, 2008, http://qando.net/details.aspx?Entry=8362.
9. Micah L. Sifry, "The Rise of the Democratic Philanthocracy," Tech-President, September 25, 2007, http://techpresident.com/blog-entry/rise-democratic-philanthocracy.
10. Peter Daou, "The Revolution of the Online Commentariat," Publius Project, December 10, 2008, http://publius.cc/2008/12/09/the-revolution-of-the-online-commentariat.

5. Fight the Right

1. "The Fox Is Wrong! (Obama Version)," Brave New Films, April 21, 2008, http://bravenewfilms.org/blog/?p=36370.

2. Joe Miller, "Corsi's Dull Hatchet," Factcheck.org, September 15, 2008, http://www.factcheck.org/elections-2008/corsis_dull_hatchet.html.
3. Julie Bosman and Jim Rutenberg, "Book Attacking Obama Hopes to Repeat '04 Anti-Kerry Feat," *New York Times*, August 12, 2008, http://www.nytimes.com/2008/08/13/us/politics/13book.html.
4. Eric H. Hananoki and Matthew Gertz, "Unfit for Publication: Corsi's *The Obama Nation* Filled with Falsehoods," Media Matters for America, August 4, 2008, http://mediamatters.org/research/200808040005.
5. "Paul Waldman Goes After Jerome Corsi and His New Book," YouTube, August 15, 2008, http://www.youtube.com/watch?v=n8foOU6n9S4.
6. Jennifer Nix, "A Tale of Two Obama Books: Why Do Progressives Still Not Get It?" Huffington Post, August 20, 2008, http://www.huffingtonpost.com/jennifer-nix/a-tale-of-two-obama-books_b_120110.html.
7. *Obama's Challenge*, http://www.obamaschallenge.org.
8. Matea Gold, "Rachel Maddow Finds the Right Formula on MSNBC," *Los Angeles Times*, September 29, 2008, http://articles.latimes.com/2008/sep/29/entertainment/et-maddow29.
9. "The Hundred Most Important Talk Show Hosts in America—Class of 2004," *Talkers Magazine Online*, http://web.archive.org/web/20041204013114/http://www.talkers.com/heavy.html.
10. Rory O'Connor, *Shock Jocks: Hate Speech and Talk Radio* (San Francisco: AlterNet Books, 2008), 222.
11. "Robert Greenwald," Internet Movie Database, 2009, http://www.imdb.com/name/nm0339254.
12. Joe Garofoli, "Fox News Critique Goes Directly to Living Rooms: Filmmakers Opt for House Parties over Theater Release," *San Francisco Chronicle*, July 19, 2004, http://www.sfgate.com/cgi-bin/article.cgi?file=/c/a/2004/07/19/MNGFV7NRTF1.DTL.
13. John Haynes and Jo Littler, "Documentary as Political Activism: An Interview with Robert Greenwald," *Cineaste* 32, no. 4 (September 22, 2007).
14. Matt Coker, "Brave New Filmmaker," *Orange County News*, June 8, 2006, http://www.ocweekly.com/2006-06-08/news/brave-new-filmmaker.
15. "About Brave New Films," Brave New Films, http://bravenewfilms.org/about.
16. Kimberley Brown, "Greenwald's Grassroots Gospel," *Realscreen*, Janu-

ary 1, 2006, http://www.realscreen.com/articles/magazine/20060101/page37.html.

17. Haynes and Littler, "Documentary as Political Activism."
18. *Wal-Mart: The High Cost of Low Price*, http://www.walmartmovie.com/wmtv.
19. Jeannette Catsoulis, "Deep Pockets in Iraq," *New York Times*, September 8, 2006, http://movies.nytimes.com/2006/09/08/movies/08prof.html.
20. William Booth, "His Fans Greenlight the Project: Robert Greenwald Tapped a New Funding Source: The Audience," *Washington Post*, August 20, 2006, http://www.washingtonpost.com/wpdyn/content/article/2006/08/18/AR2006081800210_pf.html.
21. Brave New Theaters, http://bravenewtheaters.com.
22. Steve Johnson, "Greenwald's *Iraq for Sale* Veers Off the Small-Film Path," *Chicago Tribune*, September 8, 2006, http://archives.chicagotribune.com/2006/sep/08/news/chi-0609080028sep08.
23. Fight the War on Greed, http://warongreed.org.
24. Lizzie Widdicombe, "Who's Scrooge?" *New Yorker*, December 24, 2007, http://www.newyorker.com/talk/2007/12/24/071224ta_talk_widdicombe.
25. Fox News Porn, http://foxnewsporn.com.
26. Fox Attacks, http://foxattacks.com.
27. Brave New Films, "McCain's Mansions: The Houses That Greed Built," http://bravenewfilms.org/blog/?p=49248.
28. "Keating Economics: John McCain and the Making of a Financial Crisis," http://www.keatingeconomics.com.
29. News Hounds, http://www.newshounds.us.
30. Simon Owens, "Digg Puts Focus on Politics, Bringing Charges of Liberal Bias," MediaShift, September 4, 2008, http://www.pbs.org/mediashift/2008/09/digg-puts-focus-on-politics-bringing-charges-of-liberal-bias248.html.

6. Embrace Twenty-First-Century Muckraking

1. Justin Rood, "Questions, Concerns Swirl Around Politics of Prosecutor's Forced Exit," TPM Muckracker, http://tpmmuckraker.talkingpointsmemo.com/archives/002335.php.
2. "Contributors: Seymour M. Hersh," *New Yorker*, http://www.newyorker.com/magazine/bios/seymour_m_hersh/search?contributorName=seymour%20m%20hersh.

3. Charles Lewis, "Seeking New Ways to Nurture the Capacity to Report," *Nieman Reports*, spring 2008, http://www.nieman.harvard.edu/reportsitem.aspx?id=100060.
4. Mark Briggs, *Journalism 2.0: How to Survive and Thrive: A Digital Literacy Guide for the Information Age*, ed. Jan Schaffer (Washington, DC: J-Lab: Institute for Interactive Journalism, 2007), http://www.kcnn.org/resources/journalism_20.
5. Thomas B. Edsall and Brian Faler, "Lott Remarks on Thurmond Echoed 1980 Words," *Washington Post*, December 11, 2002, http://www.washingtonpost.com/ac2/wp-dyn/A37288-2002Dec10.
6. David Kurtz, "We Knew What He Meant," Talking Points Memo, December 18, 2007, http://www.talkingpointsmemo.com/archives/061327.php.
7. David Glen, "The (Josh) Marshall Plan," *Columbia Journalism Review*, September/October 2007, http://www.cjr.org/feature/the_josh_marshall_plan.php.
8. Josh Marshall, "The Growth of Talking Points Memo and the Importance of Independent Media," keynote lecture, Park Center for Independent Media Inaugural Symposium, September 15–16, 2008, http://www.ithaca.edu/rhp/independentmedia/symposium/joshmarshall/.
9. Amram Migdal, Josh Hudelson, and Kate Redburn, "Randy 'Duke' Cunningham," TPM Muckracker, http://tpmmuckraker.talkingpointsmemo.com/cunningham.php.
10. George E. Condon Jr., "Congressman's Betrayal of Troops Called Greatest Sin: Cronies' Deals May Have Put GIs at Risk," SignOnSanDiego.com, December 1, 2005, http://www.signonsandiego.com/news/politics/cunningham/20051201-9999-1n1assess.html.
11. Randal C. Archibald, "Ex-Congressman Gets 8-Year Term in Bribery Case," *New York Times*, March 4, 2006, http://www.nytimes.com/2006/03/04/politics/04cunningham.html.
12. Justin Rood, "Cunningham Prosecutor Forced Out," TPM Muckracker, January 12, 2007, http://tpmmuckraker.talkingpointsmemo.com/archives/002329.php.
13. "Talkingpointsmemo.com's Josh Marshall on the Prosecutor Firings," *Bill Moyers Journal*, transcript, April 27, 2007, http://www.pbs.org/moyers/journal/04272007/transcript2.html.
14. Jay Carney, "Running Massacre?" Time.com, January 17, 2007, http://swampland.blogs.time.com/2007/01/17/running_massacre.

15. "TPM Canned US Attorney Scandal Timeline," Talking Points Memo, May 14, 2007, http://www.talkingpointsmemo.com/usa-timeline.php.
16. Jeff Cohen, "Josh Marshall on the Growth of Talking Points Memo and Independent Media," Huffington Post, October 3, 2008, http://www.huffingtonpost.com/jeff-cohen/josh-marshall-on-the-grow_b_131571.html.
17. Sam Apple, "Quick Off the Blog," *Financial Times*, July 28 2007, http://www.ft.com/cms/s/2/f570e4fc-397d-11dc-ab48-0000779fd2ac.html.
18. Paul Kiel, "Banned at the DOJ," Talking Points Memo, January 15, 2008, http://tpmmuckraker.talkingpointsmemo.com/2008/01/banned_at_the_doj.php.
19. Noam Cohen, "Blogger, Sans Pajamas, Rakes Muck and a Prize," *New York Times*, February 25, 2008, http://www.nytimes.com/2008/02/25/business/media/25marshall.html.
20. Josh Marshall, "Mukasey to TPM: Let's Be Friends!" Talking Points Memo, February 25, 2008, http://www.talkingpointsmemo.com/archives/179943.php.
21. Eric Alterman, "Out of Print," *New Yorker*, March 31, 2008, http://www.newyorker.com/reporting/2008/03/31/080331fa_fact_alterman?currentPage=all.
22. Josh Marshall, Talking Points Memo, April 3, 2005, http://www.talkingpointsmemo.com/archives/150655.php.
23. "Talkingpointsmemo.com's Josh Marshall on the Prosecutor Firings."
24. Josh Marshall, "TPM in 2009 and Beyond," Talking Points Memo, November 7, 2008, http://www.talkingpointsmemo.com/archives/243422.php.
25. Megan Garber, "Matt Cooper to TPM," *Columbia Journalism Review*, January 19, 2009, http://www.cjr.org/the_kicker/matt_cooper_to_tpm.php.
26. David Corn, "Who Wrecked the Economy? Foreclosure Phil," *Mother Jones*, July/August 2008, http://www.motherjones.com/politics/2008/05/foreclosure-phil.
27. "Lie by Lie: The *Mother Jones* Iraq War Timeline (8/1/90–2/14/08)," *Mother Jones*, http://www.motherjones.com/bush_war_timeline.
28. Mark Glaser, "Live-Blogging Netroots Nation's New Media Summit," MediaShift, April 17, 2009, http://www.pbs.org/mediashift/2009/04/live-blogging-netroots-nations-new-media-summit107.html.
29. Kristen Taylor, "Can Online Comments Encourage Reader Action and Support?" March 9, 2009, Knight Pulse, http://www.knightpulse.org/

blog/09/03/09/can-online-comments-encourage-reader-action-and-support.

30. Leonard Witt, "Tell Me Jay Rosen, Did Your Experiment Work?" PJNet, July 1, 2007, http://pjnet.org/post/1479.
31. Arianna Huffington, "Offthebus: Huffpost's Citizen Journalism Project Gets a Name, and Gets Rolling," Huffington Post, June 19, 2007, http://www.huffingtonpost.com/arianna-huffington/offthebus-huffposts-citiz_b_52712.html.
32. Amanda Michel, "Get Off the Bus: The Future of Pro-Am Journalism," *Columbia Journalism Review*, March/April 2009, http://www.cjr.org/feature/get_off_the_bus.php?page=all.
33. Mayhill Fowler, "Obama: No Surprise That Hard-Pressed Pennsylvanians Turn Bitter," Huffington Post, April 11, 2008, http://www.huffingtonpost.com/mayhill-fowler/obama-no-surprise-that-ha_b_96188.html.
34. Michael Tomasky, "Citizen-Journalism's Rulebook," *The Guardian*, April 15, 2008, http://www.guardian.co.uk/commentisfree/2008/apr/15/citizenjournalismsrulebook.
35. Jay Rosen, "From Off the Bus to Meet the Press," PressThink, April 15, 2008, http://journalism.nyu.edu/pubzone/weblogs/pressthink/2008/04/15/mayhill_fowler.html.
36. Jeff Jarvis, "The Press Becomes the Press-Sphere," BuzzMachine, April 14, 2008, http://www.buzzmachine.com/2008/04/14/the-press-becomes-the-press-sphere.
37. Rosen, "From Off the Bus."
38. Katharine Q. Seelye, "Blogger Is Surprised by Uproar over Obama Story, but Not Bitter," *New York Times*, April 14, 2008, http://www.nytimes.com/2008/04/14/us/politics/14web-seelye.html.
39. Carol Guensburg, "Nonprofit News," *American Journalism Review*, February/March 2008, http://www.ajr.org/Article.asp?id=4458.

7. Take It to the Hill

1. American Civil Liberties Union, "Safe and Free: Restore Our Constitutional Rights," American Civil Liberties Union, http://www.aclu.org/safefree/nsaspying/faachallenge.html.
2. "Foreign Intelligence Surveillance Act (FISA)," *New York Times*, April 16, 2009, http://topics.nytimes.com/top/reference/timestopics/subjects/f/foreign_intelligence_surveillance_act_fisa/index.html.
3. Eric Lichtblau and James Risen, "Bush Lets U.S. Spy on Callers With-

out Courts," *New York Times*, December 16, 2005, http://www.nytimes.com/2005/12/16/politics/16program.html.

4. Kristie Reilly, "Warning! You Are Being Watched," *In These Times*, September 19, 2003, http://www.inthesetimes.com/article/622.
5. Glenn Greenwald, "Response to Right-Wing Personal Attacks," Unclaimed Territory, http://glenngreenwald.blogspot.com/2006/07/response-to-right-wing-personal.html.
6. Dan Eggen, "White House Dismissed '02 Surveillance Proposal," *Washington Post*, January 26, 2006, http://www.washingtonpost.com/wp-dyn/content/article/2006/01/25/AR2006012502270.html.
7. "Hearing of the Senate Judiciary Committee: An Examination of the Call to Censure the President," Federal News Service transcript, March 31, 2006, http://www.fednews.com.
8. Glenn Greenwald, "AT&T, Other Telecoms, Buy Victory in Lawsuits," *Salon*, October 18, 2007, http://www.salon.com/opinion/greenwald/2007/10/18/rockefeller/index.html.
9. Greg Sargent, "Exclusive: Senator Chris Dodd Will Put a Hold on Telecom Immunity Bill," Talking Points Memo, October 18, 2007, http://tpmelectioncentral.talkingpointsmemo.com/2007/10/exclusive_senator_chris_dodd_will_put_a_hold_on_telecom_immunity_bill.php.
10. Duncan Black, "Hold," Eschaton, October 18, 2007, http://www.eschatonblog.com/2007_10_14_archive.html#1708094886498950587.
11. "Dodd Mania!" Digby's Hullabaloo, http://digbysblog.blogspot.com/2007/10/no-more-by-digby-dodd-mania-later-today.html.
12. Chris Bowers, "Dodd to Filibuster FISA Bill if Necessary," Open Left, October, 19, 2007, http://www.openleft.com/diary/1976/.
13. Ari Melber, "Dodd Engages the Netroots," *The Nation*, October 23, 2007, http://www.thenation.com/blogs/state_of_change/245303.
14. Shailagh Murray, "Dodd Makes Play on FISA Legislation," *Washington Post*, October 18, 2007, http://blog.washingtonpost.com/44/2007/10/18/post_137.html.
15. Jennifer Nix, "How to Create a Liberal Bestseller," *The Nation*, June 29, 2006, http://www.thenation.com/doc/20060717/nix.
16. Joe Garofoli, "Book Tops Charts Before It's Published," *San Francisco Chronicle*, May 12, 2006, http://www.sfgate.com/cgi-bin/article.cgi?f=/c/a/2006/05/12/MNG0AIQRPT1.DTL.
17. Ibid.
18. "Election '08: Talk with the Candidates," *Washington Post*, October 19,

2007, http://www.washingtonpost.com/wp-dyn/content/discussion/2007/10/04/DI2007100401628.html.

19. Tim Starks, "Senate Panel OKs Surveillance Bill," *Congressional Quarterly*, October 18, 2007, http://public.cq.com/docs/cqt/news110-000002608382.html.
20. Ryan Singel, "Democratic Lawmaker Pushing Immunity Is Newly Flush with Telco Cash," Threat Level, October 18, 2007, http://blog.wired.com/27bstroke6/2007/10/dem-pushing-spy.html.
21. "20080211 Senator Dodd Quotes Glenn Greenwald on Fisa 8:30pm," YouTube, http://www.youtube.com/watch?v=nAdj9aACgmM.
22. Greg Sargent, "MoveOn and Top Bloggers to Launch Campaign Pressuring Hillary and Obama to Back Dodd on FISA," Talking Points Memo, October 23, 2007, http://tpmelectioncentral.talkingpointsmemo.com/2007/10/moveon_to_launch_campaign_pressuring_Hillary_and_obama_to.php.
23. Greg Sargent, "Hillary Says She Would Support Filibuster of Intel Committee's Telecom Immunity Bill," Talking Points Memo, October 23, 2007, http://tpmelectioncentral.talkingpointsmemo.com/2007/10/Hillary_says_she_would_support_filibuster_of_current_bill.php.
24. Greg Sargent, "Obama Camp Says It: He'll Support Filibuster of Any Bill Containing Telecom Immunity," Talking Points Memo, October 24, 2007, http://tpmelectioncentral.talkingpointsmemo.com/2007/10/obama_camp_says_it_hell_support_filibuster_of_any_bill_containing_telecom_immunity.php.
25. Glenn Greenwald, "More Positive Steps from Democratic Candidates on the Rule of Law, Amnesty," Salon, October 24, 2007, http://www.salon.com/opinion/greenwald/2007/10/24/richardson_obama/index.html.
26. Lisa Graves, "Guest Blogger: Thoughts on the RESTORE Act, or How to Get Out of the Hole Dug When the President Pushed Through Unwise Changes to Surveillance on These Shores," ACS Blog, October 16, 2007, http://www.acslaw.org/node/11802.
27. Joe Klein, "FISA: More Than You Want to Know," Swampland, November 26, 2007, http://swampland.blogs.time.com/2007/11/26/fisa_more_than_you_want_to_kno.
28. Glenn Greenwald, "Demand Answers from *Time* Magazine," Salon, November 27, 2007, http://www.salon.com/opinion/greenwald/2007/11/27/time/index.html.
29. Klein, "FISA."

30. Rush Holt, "What's Really in the RESTORE Act," Huffington Post, November 27, 2007, http://www.huffingtonpost.com/rep-rush-holt/whats-really-in-the-rest_b_74309.html.
31. Glenn Greenwald, "*Time* Tries Again," *Salon*, November 28, 2007, http://www.salon.com/opinion/greenwald/2007/11/28/new_correction/index.html.
32. Peter Hoekstra, "Klein Kerfuffle," National Review Online, November 29, 2007, http://article.nationalreview.com/?q=OGVlNzk2YmQ4NGZjNjFhZjU4NmE0OGYyOTBhYjNiNDA=.
33. Christy Hardin Smith, "Olbermann's Special Comment on FISA," AlterNet, February 1, 2008, http://www.alternet.org/blogs/video/75707/olbermann's_special_comment_on_fisa.
34. "20080211 Senator Dodd Quotes Glenn Greenwald on FISA 8:30pm," YouTube, http://www.youtube.com/watch?v=nAdj9aACgmM.
35. American Civil Liberties Union et al., "Opposition to the FISA Legislation Proposed by Senator Bond," June 9, 2008, American Civil Liberties Union, http://www.aclu.org/pdfs/safefree/2008_june06_fisa_coalition letter.pdf.
36. Jennifer Bendery, "FISA Deal Close; Votes Could Be This Week," *Roll Call*, June 16, 2008, http://www.rollcall.com/news/25951-1.html.
37. Nick Juliano, "'Strange Bedfellows' Team up to Lobby Against Wiretap Bill," Raw Story, June 20, 2008, http://www.rawstory.com/news/2008/Strange_bedfellows_team_up_to_lobby_0620.html.
38. Jane Hamsher, "Steny Hoyer FISA Ad to Run in *Washington Post*," firedoglake, June 20, 2008, http://firedoglake.com/2008/06/20/steny-hoyer-fisa-ad-to-run-in-washington-post.
39. Glenn Greenwald, "Hoyer Hails FISA Bill as 'A Significant Victory for the Democratic Party,'" *Salon*, June 24, 2008, http://www.salon.com/opinion/greenwald/2008/06/24/hoyer/.
40. Jose Antonio Vargas, "Obama Responds to Online FISA Critics," *Washington Post*, July 3, 2008.
41. Joe Rospars, "Response from Barack on FISA and Discussion with Policy Staff," July 3, 2008, http://my.barackobama.com/page/community/post/rospars/gGxsZF.
42. Jon Pincus, "Reflections: What I Learned During My Summer Vacation," Liminal States, September 22, 2008, http://www.talesfromthe.net/jon/?p=206.
43. Ibid.
44. Carlo Scannella, "Get FISA Right: Nomadic Democracy," TechPresi-

dent, July 9, 2008, http://techpresident.com/blog-entry/get-fisa-right-nomadic-democracy.

45. Jon Pincus, "Ask the President Results (Belatedly) . . . and a Question for Harry Reid," Change.gov, April 1, 2009, http://www.change.org/ideas/28/view_blog/ask_the_president_results_belatedly_and_a_question_for_harry_reid.
46. "About The American Prospect: Our Mission," *American Prospect*, http://www.prospect.org/cs/about_tap/our_mission.
47. Sonia Smith, "Take It for Granite," Slate, January 7, 2008, http://www.slate.com/id/2181545.

8. Assemble the Progressive Choir

1. Michael Massing, "The Press: The Enemy Within," *New York Review of Books*, December 15, 2005, http://www.nybooks.com/articles/18555.
2. Scott Shane, "For Bloggers, Libby Trial Is Fun and Fodder," *New York Times*, February 15, 2007, http://www.nytimes.com/2007/02/15/washington/15bloggers.html.
3. Scarecrow, "Ykos-Libby Trial Blogging Panel," August 2, 2007, http://firedoglake.com/2007/08/02/ykos-libby-trial-blogging-panel/.
4. Cass Sunstein, "The Polarization of Extremes," *Chronicle Review*, December 14, 2007, http://chronicle.com/weekly/v54/i16/16b00901.htm.
5. Chris Bowers, "On Preaching to the Choir," MyDD, March 21, 2007, http://www.mydd.com/story/2007/3/21/182555/383.
6. Bob Ostertag, *People's Movements, People's Press: The Journalism of Social Justice Movements* (Boston: Beacon Press, 2006).
7. Victor Navasky, *A Matter of Opinion* (New York: Farrar, Straus and Giroux, 2005), 245.
8. Ibid., 142.
9. Ibid., 269.
10. "History," State Roots Project, July 7, 2006, http://www.stateroots project.org/history.
11. "Blue America Communities," Act Blue, http://www.actblue.com/page/blueamerica.
12. "America Votes 2006: U.S. Senate/Connecticut," CNN.com, http://edition.cnn.com/ELECTION/2006/pages/results/states/CT/S/01/index.html.
13. Michael M. Grynbaum, "Liberal Bloggers Come to the Fore: Websites Seen Boosting Lamont in Conn. Primary," *Boston Globe*, August

8, 2006, http://www.boston.com/news/nation/articles/2006/08/08/liberal_bloggers_come_to_the_fore.

14. David Cohn, "Jane Hamsher—FireDogLake," News Innovation, September 28, 2007, http://newsinnovation.com/2007/09/28/jane-hamsher-FireDogLake.
15. Eric Boehlert, "Bloggers Go to Bat for Obama," Media Matters for America, http://mediamatters.org/columns/200803040004.
16. "About AlterNet," AlterNet, 2009, http://www.alternet.org/about/index.html.
17. "AlterNet Books," AlterNet, 2009, https://www.alternet.org/books.

9. Move Beyond Pale, Male, and Stale

1. Howard Witt, "Blogs Help Drive Jena Protest," *Chicago Tribune*, September 18, 2007, http://www.chicagotribune.com/services/newspaper/printedition/wednesday/chi-jena_blog_web19,0,4298165.story.
2. "What Is ColorOfChange.org?" Colorofchange.org, http://colorofchange.org/about.html.
3. Chris Rabb, "Who Shall Lead?" Afro-Netizen, April 4, 2007, http://www.afro-netizen.com/2007/04/fox_attacks_oba.html.
4. Francis L. Holland, "'Afrosphere' or 'Blackroots'? Two Synonymous Names for the Same Movement," History of the AfroSpear, February 29, 2008, http://afrospear-history.blogspot.com/2008/02/afrosphere-or-blackroots-two-synonymous.html.
5. Paul Taylor and Mark Hugo Lopez, "Dissecting the 2008 Electorate: Most Diverse in U.S. History," Pew Research Center Publications, April 30, 2009, http://pewresearch.org/pubs/1209/racial-ethnic-voters-presidential-election.
6. Greenberg Quinlan Rosner Research, "Unmarried Women Change America," Women's Voices, Women's Vote, http://www.wvwv.org/research-items/unmarried-women-change-america.
7. Ruy Teixeira, "The Millennial Generation and the 2008 Election," Taking Note: A Century Foundation Group Blog, November 25, 2008, http://takingnote.tcf.org/2008/11/the-millennial-generation-and-the-2008-election.html.
8. Ruy Teixeira, "Generation We and the 2008 Election," November 17, 2008, http://futuremajority.com/files/Generation%20We%20and%202008.pdf, 11.
9. Deifell, *The Big Thaw*, vol. 2, 14.

10. Michael Tomasky, "Party in Search of a Notion," *American Prospect*, July 4, 2008, http://www.prospect.org/cs/articles?articleId=11424.
11. Jessica Clark and Tracy Van Slyke, "Welcome to the Media Revolution: How Today's Media Makers Are Shaping Tomorrow's News," *In These Times*, June 28, 2006, http://www.inthesetimes.com/article/2687.
12. Jordan Flaherty, "Racism and Resistance: The Struggle to Free the Jena Six," *Left Turn*, August 14, 2007, http://leftturn.mayfirst .org/?q=node/747.
13. Jordan Flaherty, "Justice in Jena," *Left Turn*, May 9, 2007, http://www .leftturn.org/?q=node/649.
14. Howard Witt, "Texas Denies Teen's Appeal of Conviction," *Chicago Tribune*, July 6, 2007, http://www.chicagotribune.com/services/newspaper/ premium/chi-cotton_frijul06,0,2241389.story.
15. "Chicago Tribune's Howard Witt on Power of Black Blogosphere," YouTube, http://www.youtube.com/watch?v=AZv5XxsH6ww.
16. James Rucker, "Battling Modern Day Jim Crow: the 'Jena Six': How Online Media and Activism are Making a Critical Difference," Huffington Post, August 3, 2007, http://www.huffingtonpost.com/james -rucker/battling-modern-day-jim-c_b_59048.html.
17. "Definition of the Afro-Spear," Electronic Village, June 8, 2008, http:// electronicvillage.blogspot.com/2008/06/definition-of-afrospear.html.
18. Yobachi Boswel, "Day of Blogging for Justice—Jena 6," BlackPerspec tive.net, August 30, 2007, http://www.blackperspective.net/index.php/ day-of-blogging-for-justice-jena-6.
19. Chris Kromm, "Why the 'Progressive' Blogosphere Silence About the Jena 6?" Facing South, September 20, 2007, http://www.southern studies.org/iss.
20. Pam Spaulding, "Progressive Blogosphere Mia on Jena 6," Pam's House Blend, http://www.pamshouseblend.com/showDiary.do?diaryId=3036.
21. Ann Friedman, "The Byline Gender Gap," AlterNet, October 10, 2006, http://www.alternet.org/story/42638/?page=2.
22. Jessica Clark, "She-Said/She-Said," *In These Times*, December 2, 2005, http://www.inthesetimes.com/article/2419/she_said_she_said.
23. Dana Goldstein, "Mother Tongue: Mother Jones' New Female Co-Editors on Men, Women, and Journalism," Campus Progress, February 9, 2007, http://www.campusprogress.org/features/1421/mother-tongue/ index.php?type=printer.
24. Michael Calderone, "Growing Pains for Talking Points Memo," *Politico*,

May 2, 2009, http://dyn.politico.com/printstory.cfm?uuid=F946AA5E-18FE-70B2-A8BADEEA2F4E8C43.
25. "About," Feministing.com, http://www.feministing.com/about.html#aboutFem.
26. "Mapping the Feminist Web: Presentation at Fem2pt0," Social Graph Insight, February 3, 2009, http://us.linkfluence.net/blog/?s=femisphere.
27. "Looking at Fem2pt0 and the Feminist Web," Womanist Musings, February 5, 2009, http://www.womanist-musings.com/2009/02/looking-at-fem2pt0-and-feminist-web.html.
28. Jessica Clark, "In Politics, Comedy Is Central," *In These Times*, August 4, 2006, http://www.inthesetimes.com/article/2745.
29. Stephen Duncombe, "Dreaming Up New Politics," *In These Times*, February 9, 2007.

Conclusion: What Next?

1. Jonathan Martin, "Obama Seeks Filter-Free News," *Politico*, March 24, 2009, http://dyn.politico.com/printstory.cfm?uuid=35A4B40B-18FE-70B2-A8270A160EE6690A.
2. "Baracknophobia—Obey," *Daily Show*, April 7, 2009, http://www.thedailyshow.com/watch/tue-april-7-2009/baracknophobia---obey.
3. Deifell, *The Big Thaw*, vol. 2, 30.
4. Don Hazen, "Markos 'Kos' Moulitsas on Obama, Twittering, Fighting the Blue Dogs, and the Major Changes Coming," AlterNet, May 4, 2009, http://www.alternet.org/media/139605/markos_'kos'_moulitsas_on_obama,_twittering,_fighting_the_blue_dogs,_and_the_major_changes_coming/.
5. "About," Citizen Engagement Laboratory, http://www.engagementlab.org/about.

INDEX